BECOMING
WOMEN
OF THE
WORD

"Sarah Christmyer is dazzlingly brilliant and a great writer. It's difficult for me to avoid using too many superlatives when speaking of her work and her perspicacity when it comes to the important questions of life."

Thomas Howard
Catholic literary scholar, professor, and author of *On Being Catholic*

"*Becoming Women of the Word* offers a unique blend of personal testimony, salvation history, and study of the biblical text. In this user-friendly Bible study, Christmyer introduces us to the women of the Old Testament—and to the Blessed Virgin Mary, whom they foreshadow. Christmyer presents the stories of these biblical women along with those of devout and courageous women who were her spiritual mothers in the faith. This is an excellent example of how Bible study should lead us to reflect on our own experience . . . and then to praise and thank the Lord."

Sr. Sara Butler, M.S.B.T.
Professor Emerita of Dogmatic Theology
University of St. Mary of the Lake
Mundelein, Illinois

"*Becoming Women of the Word* is more than just a rich, thoughtful, invigorating portrayal of heroines of the faith who have gone before us. It also offers practical, non-preachy takeaways of how the ancient truths these women knew can transform our often-frenetic lives today."

Ellen Vaughn
Author of *It's All About Him*

"Through biblical wisdom and relational stories, Sarah Christmyer connects us intimately with women of the Old Testament who, until now, seemed miles apart and worlds away. Reflecting on the lives of the women who walked this journey of faith before us, *Becoming Women of the Word* shows us how our beautiful gift of femininity tightly binds us together—we are all *daughters* of a King, *sisters* in Christ, and spiritual *mothers* with a powerful purpose in God's family plan. Ideal for any reading group or Bible study, this book teaches us to treasure our legacy and inspires us to pass on the faith to the next generation!"

Kelly Wahlquist
Founder of WINE: Women in the New Evangelization

"Sarah Christmyer takes us on a biblical journey with the heroines of salvation history. From Eve to Mary, we learn what it means to say yes to God's call: to have faith, to trust and hope in God's word, to wait, to pray, and to battle the devil. Christmyer makes the women of the Bible come alive for us today, and we find in their faith journeys important lessons for our own."

Edward Sri
Catholic theologian and author of *Walking with Mary*

"So often we hear in modern culture that our faith and biblical tradition is void of strong female examples and heroes. Sarah Christmyer beautifully and personally walks us through the lives of such incredible models as Ruth, Miriam, and Esther, sharing with us not only our rich heritage as modern Catholic women but also examples of true luminaries to help guide each of us on our unique paths to eternity!"

Katherine Meeks
Executive director of Endow

BECOMING
WOMEN
OF THE
WORD

HOW TO ANSWER GOD'S CALL WITH PURPOSE AND JOY

A SPIRITUAL PILGRIMAGE THROUGH THE OLD TESTAMENT

SARAH CHRISTMYER

AVE MARIA PRESS AVE Notre Dame, Indiana

© 2019 by Sarah Christmyer

Founded in 1865, Ave Maria Press is a ministry of the United States Province of Holy Cross.

www.avemariapress.com

Paperback: ISBN-13 978-1-59471-877-9

E-book: ISBN-13 978-1-59471-878-6

Cover image © Pieter-Pieter/Getty Images.

Cover and text design by Brianna Dombo.

Printed and bound in the United States of America

Library of Congress Cataloging-in-Publication Data is available.

TO MY MOTHER,
ARLITA WINSTON,
WHO SHOWED ME
WHAT IT MEANS TO BE A
WOMAN OF THE WORD,

AND TO MY DAUGHTER
AND GRANDDAUGHTER,
ABIGAIL AND GENEVIEVE SCOGNA,
TO WHOM I GRATEFULLY PASS ON
THIS LEGACY OF FAITH AND LOVE.

I am reminded of your sincere faith, a faith that dwelt first in your grandmother Lois and your mother Eunice and now, I am sure, dwells in you.

—St. Paul to Timothy in 2 Timothy 1:5

A woman who fears the Lord is to be praised. Give her of the fruit of her hands, and let her works praise her in the gates.

—Proverbs 31:30–31

CONTENTS

DAUGHTER OF GOD, REMEMBER WHO YOU ARE!

Sarah Elisabeth, what a wonderful name,
Two God-blessed women of Bible fame.
Now mother's scroll of kith and kin
Shows those like these God's grace did win.
So welcome to our family clan,
Grow strong and sweet in God's great plan
To bless some soul from day to day,
And guide them in the upward way.

—Great-Aunt Eva

When I was born, my great-aunt Eva wrote this poem, typed it onto a card she decorated with little birds, and sent it to my mother. Mom pasted it onto the front page of my baby book, where more than a half century later it continues to remind me: I am a daughter of God.

"Remember who you are!" Mom used to tell me before I left for school. Kids could call me anything they wanted to, but I always knew I had the dignity and value of being a daughter of the King of Kings, with a purpose and a place in his family plan.

I come from a long line of strong women who loved God fiercely and passed along their faith to many children, both biological and spiritual. And I am so grateful! St. Paul speaks of Timothy's "sincere faith, a faith that dwelt first in your grandmother Lois and your mother Eunice and now, I am sure, dwells in you" (2 Tm 1:5). I have that same sense, that my faith didn't start with me. I received it from people who went before me—many of whom were women.

I know my heritage is a rare and precious gift. Not everyone can say the same of their biological line. Yet just as surely as every human person comes from a biological mother, so every Christian person has been mothered spiritually, often by someone unrelated by blood. People are born, Christians are reborn. Both physical and spiritual motherhood (and fatherhood, to be sure) are central to God's plan.

"Be fruitful and multiply" (Gn 1:28) was God's charge to our first parents, a charge he repeated to Noah after the Flood (see Genesis 9:1). By the time Abraham came on the scene, it was no longer a charge but a promise: "I will make you exceedingly fruitful," God said; "and I will make nations of you, and kings shall come forth from you" (Gn 17:6). And as the blood family of Israel became fulfilled in the faith family of the Church, God brought the charge and the promise together. As Jesus told his disciples, "I chose you and appointed you that you should go and bear fruit and that your fruit should abide" (Jn 15:16).

Much has been written about the Patriarchs who sired the family of God, but no man becomes a father alone. When Jesus was born, Mary was "blessed among women." She stands in a long line of holy women who were called by God, answered his call, and prepared the world to welcome Immanuel—God with us—into our midst. As the *Catechism* tells us,

> Throughout the Old Covenant the mission of many holy women *prepared* for that of Mary. At the very beginning there was Eve; despite her disobedience, she receives the promise of a posterity that will be victorious over the evil one, as well as the promise that she will be the mother of all the living (cf. Gn 3:15, 20). By virtue of this promise, Sarah conceives a son in spite of her old age (cf. Gn 18:10–14; 21:1–2). Against all human expectation God chooses those who were considered

powerless and weak to show forth his faithfulness to
his promises: Hannah, the mother of Samuel; Deborah;
Ruth; Judith and Esther; and many other women (cf. 1
Cor 1:17; 1 Sm 1). (*CCC*, 489; emphasis in the original)

This book reflects on the lives of these Old Testament women
who said yes to God's call and found their place in his plan of
salvation. They are true women of the Word—not just because we
read about them in God's Word but also because, like the blessed
and faith-filled people of Psalm 1 and Jeremiah 17, they knew and
followed the word of God. This made them like strong trees plant-
ed by streams of water, which withstand drought and do not stop
bearing fruit. They are also women of the Word because their lives
testified to and helped prepare for the coming of Christ, the Word
himself. Like the women in my heritage, they are women of prayer
and action who balanced motherhood and work; who took up their
share in the task of being fruitful and ruling the earth.

These are ordinary women with ordinary lives. Like you and
me, they struggled with infertility or loss. They suffered; they
longed for love. They stepped into the gap when men failed them;
they worked to bring beauty from the ashes of their lives. How? In
a word: *faith*. Our spiritual mothers help us to know what faith is
and how to live it out as we too strive to hear God, say yes to his
call, and bear him to the world. Just as God has used them as part
of his plan, he can use us.

You and I are about to embark upon a kind of spiritual pilgrimage through the Old Testament, each chapter focusing on one
particular woman, and in one case, on two sisters. I feel so strongly
that their experiences are relevant to us, regardless of the miles and
years between us, that I have introduced each woman with a related story from my own life or the experience of someone who has
mothered me in faith over the years. The more things change, the
more they stay the same, someone said, and it's so true. Although
the situations some of these women found themselves in are worlds
away from what we might experience today, human nature is the
same. We face similar temptations and dilemmas as they did. But

God hasn't changed. He still calls us to follow him. And the answers provided by faith are the same.

Let's see what we can learn from the witness of those who went before us and consider how we might pass on the faith, in our turn, as women of the Word and mothers of faith ourselves.

QUESTIONS FOR REFLECTION

- Who has been your Lois or Eunice, a spiritual mother in your life? How did she pass her faith on to you?
- If this mother of faith is alive today, how can you thank her?
- "Just as God has used [the women of the Old Testament] as part of his plan, he can use [you]." Which biblical woman are you most looking forward to learning more about? Why?

EVE

IN THE BEGINNING, THERE WAS LOVE

At the very beginning there was Eve; despite her disobedience, she receives the promise of a posterity that will be victorious over the evil one, as well as the promise that she will be mother of all the living (cf. Gn 3:15, 20).
—*Catechism of the Catholic Church*, 489

The LORD God said to the serpent, . . .
"I will put enmity between you and the
    woman,
    and between your seed and her seed;
he shall bruise your head,
    and you shall bruise his heel."
—Genesis 3:14, 15

I have had faith in Christ for as long as I can remember. According to the Protestant tradition in which I was raised, I asked Jesus into my heart when I was small. I learned the books of the Bible along with the alphabet, memorized verses for Sunday school, argued theology with my brothers while doing the dishes. Except for several years while I was in middle school, we went regularly to church. I learned to read the Bible, pray, and turn my troubles over to God.

I went through some typical teenage faltering, but I never really rebelled.

In time, I got married. Mark and I were happy at first. We had good careers, our dream house, and no worries to speak of. But a year later, all of that changed. There was no job, no house, and we were sinking deep into debt. My grandfather died, my mother got cancer, and my world began falling apart. I remember curling up in a ball on the kitchen floor and crying out to God, "How could this happen? Why don't you save us?"

If I ever needed to draw on the resources of faith, it was then. But ironically—or maybe it was by the grace of God—at the same time, I was going through a real internal crisis. After several years of attending my Presbyterian church, Mark had decided to revert to the Catholic faith of his childhood. I was terrified. The little I knew about Catholics had convinced me that the Catholic Church put barriers in the way of a personal relationship with Christ. How could I raise my children with that influence in their lives?!

I joined RCIA[1] to find reasons *not* to be Catholic, so I could dissuade Mark. My journey opened a rift with my family, who didn't understand. Protestant friends drifted away. Worst of all, as I tried to sift through the theology and figure out what was true, what had once felt like a strong rock beneath me began to shift. I fell into a kind of limbo of nonbelonging, loneliness, and fear.

One day in prayer, I heard God ask me, *Who brought you here?* Well, I sure didn't get there myself! I threw my hurt, fear, and anger at God until there was nothing left to throw. Then it was as if his hand stretched out to me. *I'm going this way,* he said. *Are you coming?* I felt no judgment from him, only love.

At the time, I took his question to mean I should pursue becoming Catholic. And when I did that, I found—to my surprise—I didn't have to abandon my faith; rather, I found a richness and fullness within this new tradition that I didn't expect.

Looking back, I realize that "going this way" was about more than Church membership. It also meant responding to God's loving invitation and trusting his work in my life. I decided to take God's hand that day, even though the way wasn't clear and I was terrified. I felt like the disciples in John 6 after Jesus told them they had to eat his flesh and many of his followers left. Jesus asked if they were going to leave too. "Lord, to whom shall we go? You have the words of eternal life; and we have believed, and have come to know, that you are the Holy One of God" (Jn 6:68–69).

That is faith in its essence, I think. The *Catechism* puts it this way: "Faith is first of all a personal adherence of man to God" (*CCC*, 150). Faith is entrusting ourselves wholly, completely, to the God who loves us. It's believing him absolutely—even if we don't yet sense the truth of what he says, even if we can't see the path ahead.

Pope Benedict XVI writes that "faith [is] the acceptance, filled with wonder and gratitude, of the unprecedented divine initiative that precedes us and summons us."[2]

Think about that—the Lord is seeking a relationship with you before you even think about him. Like the hand I saw extended to me all those years ago, God makes an offer of love to each one of us. How have you experienced that in your life? Is he calling to you now in some way? Faith is accepting that offer—even if it means holding his hand in the dark.

GETTING THE CONTEXT

There's a whole chapter in Hebrews devoted to the value of living by faith. It goes through the Old Testament, naming people who pleased God, or who were saved or blessed, or who endured persecution or martyrdom—all because of their unshakable faith.

Two names are strangely absent from that chapter: our first parents are not mentioned in that "roll call of the faithful," as Hebrews 11 is sometimes called. (It begins with their son Abel.) It's Adam and Eve who first lost their trust in the Father. They are the reason we were separated from God and even today find ourselves struggling to answer his call to love.

The story of Eve intrigues me. Her name comes from the Hebrew *hawwa*, "to live." By naming her Eve, Adam recognized her as "the mother of all living" (Gn 3:20). She is the earthly mother of us all. From her comes a legacy of life that knows it's made for more. She may have lost her trust initially, resulting in the Fall, but she also picked up afterward and moved forward on the strength of God's promise. How did she do that? What can we learn from her?

Let's go back to the Garden of Eden, to the beginning of time. The long line of women that leads us to Mary is anchored in the legacy of Eve.

EVE'S STORY

You can read about Eve in Genesis 1:1–5:5.

Eve woke up to love.

What must that have been like? Her experience was very different from that of Adam, who opened his eyes to work, to the God-given tasks of tilling and keeping the garden, to naming the animals and learning rules to live by. In the process, he discovered his need for another who couldn't be found. Life was good, beautiful even, but Adam was alone. And that was the one, not-good thing about the good world God had created.

But Eve—created specially by God to solve that one, not-good thing—woke up to love. To completeness. *To relationship.*

I envision Eve opening her eyes for the very first time and seeing before her the loving face of her Creator. I see him smile with loving approval. She was a beauty! He held out his hand and took her to Adam (see Genesis 2:22).

Uniting the two seems to have been the first order of business. God and Eve didn't detour through the garden to admire the roses; they didn't stop to pet a passing fawn. Eve would receive her knowledge of paradise from the man she was *made for* in the best sense of that phrase. The first thing she knew about herself was that she was a gift. She was someone created by God and meant for Adam. She was a helpmeet, a "helper fit for him" (Gn 2:18).

Do you find yourself cringing at Eve being a "helpmeet"? Despite the English connotations of that word, God didn't create Eve to be a doormat for her husband. The Hebrew is *'ezer kenegdo*. Jewish scholar Robert Alter translates it as "sustainer beside him."[3]

In the Psalms, *'ezer* is used for God as one who delivers, protects, and upholds life.[4] In John's gospel, Jesus uses the Greek equivalent of the word to describe the Holy Spirit, the "Counselor" or helper he sends to be with us in his absence.[5]

Clearly Eve wasn't a lowly sidekick but someone whom Adam really needed, who had strengths that Adam didn't. Like Adam, she was like God. She wasn't a subordinate but a partner. Eve was an indispensable companion in fulfilling the will of God.

I expect that Eve knew right away how much she was loved and appreciated, because when Adam saw her, he didn't respond as if he had finally found the help he needed. It was more like, "Where have you been all my life?!"

"This at last is bone of my bones and flesh of my flesh" (Gn 2:23), he cried. Woo-hoo! He had spent his whole life so far tending the garden, coaxing fruit from the vines and planting trees down by the river where they could flourish. He had been naming the animals, discovering all the wonders of God's creation. But in Eve he saw something new! Hers was a beauty far beyond that of the sky or any other creature. Adam took one look at Eve and his heart was hers. In that instant he knew he was created for more than just work. He was created to love.

Adam and Eve stood before God, and God blessed them and their union. He charged them to be fruitful and fill the earth with their children, to care for the earth and its creatures. Eve must have taken a good look at the delights around her as God continued. This was to be their home! Having blessed the first couple, God gifted them with everything they would need. And he saw that "it was very good" (Gn 1:31).

LOVE IS SHATTERED BY DOUBT

The Bible is silent about what happened after Adam and Eve met, but there must have been time for the newlyweds to get acquainted, time for Adam to fill Eve in on what he learned from God before she got there. Presumably he showed her around the garden and told her that God gave them every tree to eat—"but of the tree of the knowledge of good and evil you shall not eat, for in the day that you eat of it you shall die" (Gn 2:17). He must have shown her that tree and impressed on her its importance.

I suspect he introduced her to the animals as well and told her their names and how those names reflected each one's essence. *That one I called serpent*, I can hear Adam saying. *Listen to it hiss. . . . Watch out for that one, now.*[6]

I'm imagining that conversation, of course, but scripture is clear: God gave the command about the tree to Adam *before* he created Eve (see Genesis 2:16–18). So when the serpent sidled in and said to the woman, "Did God say, 'You shall not eat of any tree of the garden?'" (Gn 3:1)—how did she know what God said unless she heard it from Adam? And was the serpent questioning God's word or Adam's reliability?

We can't eat from that one tree, Eve said, *or even touch it—or we'll die* (see Genesis 3:3). It's hard to know if Adam told her that, or if she embellished the command. But the serpent called the whole thing a lie. "You will not die," it said. "For God knows that when you eat of it your eyes will be opened, and you will be like God, knowing good and evil" (Gn 3:4–5).

If it wasn't good for Adam to be alone, it wasn't good for Eve to be alone either. She didn't look to Adam for help; she listened to the serpent. I can see her pause to think. *What if the serpent was right?* Maybe God was withholding something good. Maybe Adam lied. Whom was she going to believe?

So Eve went right up to the tree and took a piece of fruit in her hand to check it out for herself.

Here's where I relate to Eve. The fruit was "a delight to the eyes" (Gn 3:6)—and I love beauty. I've been known to drive off the road under the influence of the sun setting on a mountain range. I can't find my way through the woods because I get too distracted by moss and mushrooms (looking at them, not eating them!). When something is particularly beautiful, I can get almost sick with wanting it. Never mind if it's too expensive or somehow bad for me.

Eve faced a triple threat. The fruit was beautiful; she saw it would taste good; and the serpent told her it would make her wise. That pretty well sums up the temptations to sin that the world imposes upon us: the lust of the flesh, the lust of the eyes, and the pride of life (see 1 John 2:16).

It was all too much to resist. Eve took another look at the tree and forgot all the good things God had given them. She had eyes only for that tree, and she wanted it. It was the word of the serpent against the word of God and the word of Adam, and she went with the serpent. She took the fruit and ate; and she gave some to Adam, and he ate too.

The *Catechism* describes what happened: "Man, tempted by the devil, let his trust in his Creator die in his heart and, abusing his freedom, disobeyed God's command" (*CCC*, 397).

When trust dies in your heart, what happens to love? In my experience, it flies out the window. Adam and Eve preferred the lies of the serpent to the words of the One who loved them. They disobeyed God's word, they lost trust in his goodness, and they exalted themselves over God and therefore chose against their own good.

GOD'S LOVE HANGS IN FOR THE LONG HAUL

Those choices had consequences. Adam and Eve (and their descendants) became subject to suffering and death. They still bore God's image; they were still called to be fruitful and multiply and govern the earth. But all those things would be marred by pain and labor and would be carried out *outside* of Eden. And where desire between the man and woman once led to a mutual self-giving, now there would be domination. Eve's desire would be for her husband, but Adam—instead of ruling the earth with his partner at his side— would rule over her.

This isn't how we were created to be; it's a damnable result of the Fall.

God could have left things as is, I suppose. Like the cosmic clockmaker some people imagine him to be, he could have brushed off his hands and started fresh somewhere else. But love doesn't give up. God cursed the serpent, and then declared war.

God said to the serpent, "I will put enmity between you and the woman, and between your seed and her seed; he shall bruise [or "crush," as the same word is translated in Job 9:17] your head, and you shall bruise his heel" (Gn 3:15).

In other words, in an ongoing battle that is within the providence of God and his loving plan, the serpent will continue to work against people and even harm them. That is the "bruised heel" God spoke of. But a seed (descendant) of the woman will crush the serpent's head. The woman who was deceived will be the key to making things right. And not just the woman; the woman *and her seed*. Normally we speak of the man as having seed and the woman as receiving it. It's mysterious here, but we see that it's not a woman as an individual who is involved but rather a woman and her child who will be victorious.

EVE'S DOUBT DISSOLVES IN HOPE

The way the Bible tells it, Eve took God at his word and began looking for that promised "seed" and savior. She had a son and named him Cain, "saying, 'I have gotten a man with the help of the LORD'" (Gn 4:1). Notice that she still had a relationship with God and with Adam, however damaged those relationships might be. She and Adam were still intimate. And Eve, rather than being estranged from the God she betrayed, saw him as "the LORD" who helped make her fruitful. She went on to become "the mother of all living" (Gn 3:20).

Before the Fall, Eve doubted God's word. After the Fall, she hoped in his promise.

But Cain wasn't the promised "seed." In a fit of jealous rage, he killed his brother Abel and was banished. Putting myself in Eve's place, if I lost my first two sons that way, I might not try for another. Why continue to "be fruitful and multiply" if the result is murder and death? But see the growing faith of Eve: in Genesis 4:25, she bore another son and called him *Seth*, which means "given" or "appointed." For "God has appointed for me another child instead of Abel, for Cain slew him," she said.

It's an interesting word choice. Eve saw in her son someone *appointed* by God, as to a role in his plan. She wasn't overcome by despair but rather filled with hope. Here was another son, another seed from God. Maybe he would overcome the devil and the curse that plagued them!

Seth didn't overcome the devil in that way, but with his line, "men began to call upon the name of the LORD" (Gn 4:26). Genesis traces Seth's family line to Noah, who was expected to bring relief from their work and toil on the cursed ground (Gn 5:29). The promise lived on! And from Noah's son Shem came another family line that led to Abraham, whose wife was Sarah: two who would father and mother the people of God. From that people would come a new Eve and a second Adam, Mary and Jesus, the promised woman and her seed who would definitively crush the head of the serpent. Along the way, prefiguring that woman, came the women we will meet in the rest of this book.

CLAIMING EVE'S LEGACY:
THE TRIUMPH OF LOVE

Fast-forward to Holy Saturday, AD 33.

Eve once again woke up to love, this time from the grave.

Her eyes opened on the face of God the Son—who had died on the Cross, descended into the realm of the dead, and triumphantly thrown open its gates for the souls awaiting their savior.[7] Here at last was the promised "seed of the woman." How Eve must have rejoiced to see him!

Christ's descent to deliver the dead so they can rise to heaven has traditionally been called the "harrowing of hell," or *anastasis* in Greek. Some Christian art shows them released from graves; others depict them snatched from the jaws of a monstrous beast reminiscent of the serpent. Most show Jesus offering his hands first to Adam and Eve. They emerge from death leading the righteous dead. All those years ago in Eden, God brought the newly created Eve to his "son," Adam. Now *the* Son, Jesus, brings Eve, bursting with new and eternal life, back to the Father. In that outstretched hand I see the one he offered me. I hear again, *Are you coming?*

People tend to have one-sided pictures of Eve. They see her as the original temptress, the cause of the Fall for us all. Or they see her as weak and cursed with pain in childbirth and subjected to domination by men. Some people see all women in that way. But even if you feel like that sometimes, God cursed the serpent, not Eve; and he featured the woman in his promise. The effects of the Fall are not a curse from God but a state from which he wants to free us. It's up to us to respond, in love and faith.

Our picture of Eve isn't complete without what she did after the Fall. Eve didn't let guilt defeat her. She grabbed onto God's promise and didn't let go. She acted on it, continuing to do her part to bear the promised "seed," even when the first was wicked and the second one died. She didn't give up when the picture was bleak. How was she able to do that, unless she knew God's love was stronger than her sin?

Know that you are loved, like Eve, and that nothing will stop God from loving you. If you have out-and-out defied him as Eve did—he went to death to get you back. Turn around and you will see his outstretched hand. If you have wandered off, he's looking for you. If you're lost and confused, as I was, stop and listen. His love is calling: *Are you coming? Come and see. Follow me.*

Eve gives me hope. I struggle because of the Fall. But that doesn't mean that I am damned. God loves me and remains faithful when I am not. Jesus stands ready to pull me from the graves I wander into. He has conquered the serpent and set me free. He stands there with his forgiveness. And Eve, from heaven, cheers me on.

QUESTIONS FOR REFLECTION

- What in Eve's story or the author's faith journey resonates with you? How have you experienced something similar?
- Today, in what particular way is God saying to you, *Are you coming?*
- What serpent in your life is making it difficult for you to trust? Can you ask the Lord for the grace you need to follow the way he is leading? Write out your prayer.

SARAH

GOD CALLS US TO TRUST

By faith Sarah herself received power to conceive, even when she was past the age, since she considered him faithful who had promised.

—Hebrews 11:11

It's funny how traits pass down through families. There's a photo of my grandma Grace framed on the wall of my dining room; people often remark on the resemblance between us. It's not just our faces. She was tall, lean, and reserved like I am. Grace must have seen something of herself in me, because she sat me down one day to warn me against falling for a young man who needed "saving." She'd almost made that mistake once, canceling the wedding and sending back all the gifts just weeks before the big day. She suffered a lot of heartache before meeting her true love, my grandfather, John.

John had done relief work in Europe during World War I with the American Friends Service Committee.[1] While he was there, he felt God call him to missionary work. Grace shared John's vision. Soon after they married, the young couple packed their bags and headed overseas with the Belgian Gospel Mission. Not everyone appreciated their decision, least of all their families. John had been groomed his whole life to take over the family publishing business. From the outside, they seemed to be throwing everything away— status, money, prospects, friends—all for something that would return little beyond the satisfaction of serving the Lord. Surely that could be done through charitable works at home, without giving up so much!

But leave they did. Grace was smart, articulate, and saw herself making a real difference in Belgium through her teaching and writing. And so it came as a hard surprise when she felt the Lord asking her to set aside her dreams and stay home with her boys. *I need you to pray*, she heard God say. She was being called away from the active life to a contemplative one, to partner with God in the quiet of her prayer closet.

Years later, Grandma spoke of her struggle, of what it meant to have gifts and to choose not to use them. To feel barren and unproductive. In the end, she chose to obey what she heard from the Lord. To die to herself and to follow the calling of God.

It's nice to think of God's hand outstretched to us, but the truth is, we don't always know what he's calling us to or the path it will take to get there. His ways are not ours. Sometimes his way leads into the dark. It might require us to leave what we love behind. Other times, it asks the impossible. Do we trust God's love enough to follow him? That is the question.

I think of Grace as I start into the story of Sarah in Genesis 12. "Leave your world behind and go to a place where I will show you," God instructed her husband, Abraham (see Genesis 12:1). Together they left everything: family, country, the gods of their ancestors. Empty, they followed God into the unknown.

GETTING THE CONTEXT

Now the LORD said to Abram, "Go from your country and your kindred and your father's house to the land that I will show you. And I will make of you a great nation, and I will bless you and make your name great, so that you will be a blessing. . . . And by you all the families of the earth shall bless themselves." (Gn 12:1–3)

This promise was directed to Abraham, but it was made equally to his wife, Sarah. She is the first woman after Eve to be described in any detail. Her importance in salvation history is related to the child she will bear, who will be first in a long line of the promised "seed of the woman"[2] who become the family of God.

I am struck by the contrast between Sarah's emptiness and the strength of the legacy she left behind. She was completely barren—infertile and way past menopause—yet she is remembered as the mother of nations and is held up by prophets and saints as a model of inner beauty, faith, and courage.[3] This gives me hope! When I feel insufficient or empty, not up to the task, Sarah shows me that waiting is worthwhile and that there's something about human emptiness that gives God a place in which to plant his life.

SARAH'S STORY

You can read about Sarah in Genesis 11:27–12:20; Genesis 16:1–18:15; and Genesis 20–23.

Sarah and Abraham—or Sarai and Abram, as they were known at first—were old and settled when God's call came. Their family was deeply rooted in Ur of the Chaldees, a powerful city not far from the Persian Gulf in the country we know as Iraq. Abram heard God's voice and decided to gather his family and follow. He went as far as Haran, about six hundred miles northwest of Ur in modern-day Turkey, and stayed until the death of his father. When Abram was seventy-five and Sarai was sixty-five years old, they ventured into Canaan.

Abram was well-off, with plenty of servants and possessions. What he and Sarai lacked was children. It's curious that Abram had never sought another wife, given the importance then of having an heir. But Sarai was a real beauty (see Genesis 12:11, 14). Her name means "my princess" or "ruler," and Jewish tradition praises her as a model of excellence. Abram must have really loved her, not to seek a child from someone else.

The Bible doesn't tell us what Sarai did for the half century before this part of the story begins. I wonder what she did with that empty space she must have felt. Where did she direct her longing? In a day when a woman's worth was wrapped up in having sons and heirs, how did she hold her head high? And how long did she keep that space lined, in her mind, like a nest, soft and ready for the child who didn't come? When did she give up and move on? I can't imagine that in her mid-sixties she continued to hope for children. However painful that hole in her life and heart might have been earlier on, that door was closed.

In rabbinic tradition, Sarah is known for her wisdom. It's said that she taught the women about the one God as Abraham taught the men.[4] Even today she is hailed as one of seven female prophets in the Old Testament.[5] It seems she lived a settled life, respected and surrounded by family, with a faithful husband, servants to help with the burdens of housework, and time to minister to her spiritual daughters.

SARAH FOLLOWS GOD

What did Sarai think when Abram told her they were to leave all that behind? The older I get, the more I appreciate the value of someplace familiar to call home and the nearness of family to share the burdens of life. There's a reason age sixty-five is considered retirement age! By that point, most people are ready to hunker down and stay in one place.

But Abram picked up and went, and Sarai went with him. To leave her family and everything she knew to go to an unknown location, relying on God to tell Abram what to do—that must have been scary. But there's no indication that she was afraid. St. Peter, it seems, agrees: "You are now [Sarah's] children," he says to Christians of the early Church, "if you do right and let nothing terrify you" (1 Pt 3:6).

That ability not to fear what is frightening stood Sarai in good stead. Because almost at once, they faced temptation. It turns out that not only was Sarai barren but the Promised Land was barren too. Facing famine, they walked right through Canaan to Egypt. But before they entered, Abram realized that the local rulers were likely to desire Sarai for themselves, because of her beauty; they might even kill him to have her. He made his wife promise to say she was his sister, whereupon Pharaoh took her for himself, which threatened God's plan to start a new family with Abram and Sarai.

There are echoes here of the Fall. The symbol of Egypt is the serpent. Abram put Sarai in the lap of Pharaoh, then stood by, saying nothing—not protecting or even acknowledging his bride. Sarai was left facing the serpent alone. But God was with her.

At the Fall, Eve succumbed to the lure of the serpent, who tempted her to doubt God's goodness and the sufficiency of what he had given to them. She wanted more, and on her own terms. Now this daughter of Eve found herself like a wife to Pharaoh, a position that brought with it gifts and privileges—blessing from someone other than God. Coincidence? Instead of grasping for more, as Eve did, Sarai risked her life and that of her husband to leave Pharaoh and return with Abram to the land of seeming famine, to the place of God's promise.

SARAH BARGES AHEAD

Sarai was a woman of faith who acted on her hope in God. But that didn't lessen the odds against achieving what God promised. To inherit the land and become a great nation, Abram and Sarai needed a child. And although ten more years passed, Sarai didn't conceive.

It's easy to understand what happened next. All those years, they'd been monogamous, faithful. They knew God meant for them to have descendants. But they were old and barren, and God hadn't given them a child. So Sarai did what many people in that time and place would have done: she gave Abram her Egyptian servant Hagar "as a wife" with the understanding that any son from their union would be considered Sarai and Abram's. Abram listened to Sarai's voice (see Genesis 16:2–3). But in her voice was the voice of the serpent who sought to prevent the royal, promised seed.

Hagar promptly became pregnant, which is what everyone wanted, except that in consequence, "[Hagar] looked with contempt on her mistress" (Gn 16:4). This was more than Sarai could bear. She hurled her anger at Abram: "May the wrong done to me be on you! . . . May the LORD judge between you and me!" (Gn 16:5).

There's no way to sugarcoat Sarai's reaction. She retaliated so harshly that Hagar fled. But God was good to Hagar. He met her in the wilderness and encouraged her to return, which she did, secure in the knowledge that she was noticed and looked after by God.

Hagar is one of the "hidden" women of the Bible. She seems to be of little consequence, given that it was decidedly *not* her seed line that would produce the Messiah. In the biblical text, neither Abram nor Sarai even called her by name; but God did, and he allowed her to see him and he blessed her child. Because of Hagar we know that about God, that he is "a God of seeing" who sees our troubles and tends to us—even those of us who feel unimportant, mistreated, or discarded like this poor Egyptian slave.

Hagar bore Abram a son he called *Ishmael*, which means "God hears." Sarai's plan had succeeded. Did she slowly resign herself to this, in spite of her difficult relationship with Hagar? It seems so. They must all have assumed that God's promise would be fulfilled through Ishmael. However, God had something else in mind.

SARAH TRUSTS GOD'S PLAN

When Abram was ninety-nine, the Lord appeared to him again. Ishmael was thirteen and on the cusp of adulthood. God confirmed his promises and gave Abram a new name: *Abraham*, "father of a multitude of nations." Then came the twist: God said, "I will bless [Sarai], and moreover I will give you a son by her. I will bless her, and she shall be a mother of nations; kings of peoples shall come from her" (Gn 17:15–16). To underscore the promise, God gave Sarai a new name too; she would be *Sarah*, "Princess."

Name changes in the Bible indicate a new mission and destiny. There doesn't seem to be much difference between Sarai ("my princess") and Sarah ("Princess"). But notice that God changed both Sarai's and Abram's names by adding the letter *h*. According to the Jewish mystics, the Hebrew letter *h* (*hey*) represents the divine breath and gift of life. It's the root of the verb *haya*, which means "being." It also signifies grace and God's divine work in the world. Alone, it means "behold!"

In a way, by changing their names God was announcing, *Behold, the father of nations! . . . Behold, a princess and mother of kings!* God was doing something new in them.

That God would determine to bless Sarah with children seemed so preposterous given their advanced age (Sarah was ninety) that Abraham fell on his face and laughed. What else could he do? You can see the tears running down his face: "Come on, Lord. What about Ishmael? Isn't he enough? Can't you fulfill your plans through him?" (see Genesis 17:18). God said, "No, but Sarah your wife shall bear you a son, and you shall call his name Isaac. I will establish my covenant with him as an everlasting covenant for his offspring after him. As for Ishmael, I have heard you; behold, I will bless him. . . . But I will establish my covenant with Isaac, whom Sarah shall bear to you at this season next year" (Gn 17:19–21).

He couldn't get much clearer than that. The son of the promise would be Sarah's firstborn, not Abraham's. And his name would be Isaac, which means "laughter"! His name will be a permanent reminder that God can do the impossible, an encouragement to have faith even when the situation is laughable.

The Lord then told Sarah the news. In the form of three strangers, he visited the couple at their tent. Abraham rushed out to serve them, and when they settled down to their food, they asked for Sarah, who was listening from inside. "I'll be back this time next year," the Lord said, "and your wife Sarah will have a son" (see Genesis 18:10). She reacted as Abraham had, laughing to herself. And God heard her.

> The Lord said to Abraham, "Why did Sarah laugh and say, 'Shall I indeed bear a child, now that I am old?' Is anything too hard for the Lord? At the appointed time I will return to you, in the spring, and Sarah shall have

> a son." But Sarah denied, saying, "I did not laugh"; for
> she was afraid. He said, "No, but you did laugh." (Gn
> 18:13–15)

Knowing that Sarah laughed at God's promise, I struggle to see how the author of Hebrews can speak of the strength of her faith. But Pope Benedict XVI says this verse shows that "the entire redemptive initiative comes from God, from his grace, from his forgiveness received in faith."[6] Sarah shows us that our faith is made possible by God's gracious gift.

As promised, Isaac was born the following year. Imagine their joy!

The day he was weaned, probably two or three years later, Abraham threw a feast in his honor. Sarah saw Ishmael playing with her son and she wasn't amused. What was wrong with Ishmael playing with the child? In Hebrew, the word used for playing is literally "laughing." It's the same word Sarah used to name her baby. Ishmael was laughing at Isaac, the boy whose name means "laughter." His was a counterfeit, mocking laughter from a counterfeit heir. Maybe Ishmael was messing with the younger boy, as some commentaries say. But maybe he was trying to be "laughter"; trying to "out Isaac" Isaac and cut in on God's promise.

Whatever Hagar's son was doing, it didn't go over well with Sarah. Her reaction was decisive and instant. "Cast out this slave woman with her son," she demanded of Abraham; he "shall not be heir with my son Isaac" (Gn 21:9–10). Perhaps realizing the awesome responsibility that she and Abraham had been given by God to be the father and mother of nations through Isaac, she acted to remove the competition. Abraham wasn't happy about it. He loved both boys. But God's promise was to go through Sarah's son, Isaac. It was he who would inherit the patriarchal responsibilities of the family after Abraham. God told Abraham to listen to his wife. God himself would take care of Hagar and Ishmael; Abraham and Sarah were to focus on Isaac.

Given all this, it's hard to imagine the faith it took for Abraham, a number of years later, to obediently offer up that promised son upon an altar (see Genesis 22). Scripture says nothing about what Sarah felt or did when God made that terrible demand. Did she even know where the men were going when they left early that morning, and why? If so, what was it like to know her son suffered because of faithful obedience to God? Did she share in Abraham's belief that God who gave them this son could also restore him to life (see Hebrews 11:19)?

This story hints at one that will play out in Jerusalem two thousand years later, when Mary would suffer, watching her Son die on a Cross. Both women ultimately experienced God's presence within their pain. The God who brought life from a barren womb and raised it from an altar, promising a lamb in his place, would bring life from a virgin womb, offer it as *the* lamb and raise it from a tomb. God is in the business of bringing life. Death *does not* have the last word.

CLAIMING SARAH'S LEGACY: GOD MAKES US FRUITFUL IN HIS TIME

So much of faith is about waiting. We wait on God to act. We wait for him to answer our prayers. We wait to learn his will, to feel his presence in our lives. As I write this chapter, I'm waiting on a prognosis from my doctor. How deep is the melanoma he discovered? How far has it intruded into my lymph system? Can they cut it out, like a bruise from an apple—or is it too late? It's the limbo that's hard, the not knowing what lies ahead. I can't stop my mind from racing. What will this mean for me and my family? It could mean suffering, even death—or just a couple of scars. I cry out for the grace I need for today and ask that that be enough, that I not yearn for what I don't need, but rest in the Lord's loving care. *Jesus, I trust in you. Jesus, I trust . . .*

In my waiting, I find myself turning to Sarah, who lived in the not-knowing for a lifetime. She may not have had a disease to wonder about, but there was that call that led into the dark—like that call that led my grandma Grace into a chosen obscurity. With Abraham, Sarah left behind a world of human possibility and set off for the unknown in a land that seemed stripped of potential. With Abraham, she waited for an heir . . . for decades. She also struggled with doubt. How can blessing come from a sterile, unproductive place? I expect Grandma Grace wondered the same thing. And why would God make Sarah wait so long to see what he had promised?

Perhaps that is the point. That in this woman who will be the matriarch—the "quarry" from which God's family will be dug, to use the image used for her in Isaiah 51:1—there must be something of the very essence of the faith that will mark those who follow God. Faith hangs on even when the situation looks impossible, because faith knows God can be trusted.

The more I read Sarah's story, the more it stands out to me that God wanted her—and only her—to be the mother of his people. Specifically, he wanted his family to come from a woman who couldn't have those children by herself but who needed his help, from someone who had to trust that God was able to bring life and that he would do as he promised (Heb 11:11). Sarah's life shows the triumph of God's power over the human limitation and doubt that had reigned since the Fall. God was starting a new family that would bless the entire world. To do so, it had to be clear that membership in that family would come by faith in him.

That lesson about faith has to do with fruitfulness as well. We all want to be fruitful in some way, whether that means having our own children or helping others thrive or having a fruitful ministry or somehow making a difference in the world. I think of Grandma Grace, staying home and praying when there was so much work to be done, when she'd rather be out teaching and writing. She shifted her focus from public ministry to investing in her sons, she prayed for the needs of the mission, and she let God worry about what fruit would come. Decades later she told me she was amazed at what had blossomed as a result of her prayers and from the investment she made in her children. She had no regrets at all.

When I feel unproductive or barren, Sarah gives me hope. She had just one son, and so late in life. But her legacy is as a *matriarch*. A mother of many. Those "many" aren't just the Jewish people. Some were women she introduced to the one God. Others are transplants like you and me. We plant and water, but it's God who gives the growth (see 1 Corinthians 3:6). We must trust that it will come in his time and in his way.

Postscript: The doctors were successful in removing all of the melanoma, and it has not, as far as they can determine, entered farther into my lymph system. I am enormously grateful and, at the same time, aware in a new way of the fragility of life and the need (and value) of faith.

QUESTIONS FOR REFLECTION

- What in Grace's journey or Sarah's story resonates with you? How have you experienced something similar?
- When, if ever, have you felt like Hagar, cast into the wilderness and unable to obtain justice for those you love? What does her story say to you?
- In what particular way is God calling you to leave something behind or trust him today?
- What did you learn from this chapter that might give you patience or strengthen your faith?

LEAH AND RACHEL

GOD LONGS TO FILL OUR HEARTS

May the LORD make the woman, who is coming into your house, like Rachel and Leah, who together built up the house of Israel.

—Ruth 4:11

My middle name—Elisabeth—comes from my great-great-aunt Elsebeth, but Mom changed the spelling in honor of her good friend Elisabeth Elliot. Betty, as my parents called her, grew up in Belgium with my dad. Their parents were missionaries together, and during World War II the families lived on the same street in New Jersey. Most of their kids went to the same small boarding school that my mom went to, in Florida; then they all trooped off to Wheaton College in Illinois. The shared experiences of a lifetime have made us family.

In the mid-1950s, Elisabeth's husband, Jim, and four other missionaries were speared to death when they tried to contact people of the Auca tribe in Ecuador. Elisabeth later returned with their young daughter and lived with that same tribe for two years. *Life* magazine told the story.[1] Although the published reports make her sound heroic, she felt anything but.

One evening after returning to America, Betty stood in our kitchen washing dishes as my mother dried them and put them away. She told about the great losses she'd experienced early on as a missionary, even before she was married. For an entire year, she had painstakingly worked to get the language of the Ecuadorian indigenous group the Colorados into an alphabet so a translation could be made of the Bible. One day she heard gunshots outside her little house in the jungle, followed by a great commotion. She looked into the yard and saw a Colorado man standing over the body of Don Macario, her translator, whom he had shot point-blank in the head.[2]

As far as Elisabeth knew, that translator was the only person in the world who knew both Spanish and the Colorado language. He had been a huge answer to her prayers and confirmation of her mission. How could this happen? Not long after, she gathered her precious notes and papers together and caught a bus to town. The bus was crowded, and the driver tied Elisabeth's little suitcase to the top, along with cages of chickens, crated vegetables, and other goods destined for the market. The bus jolted down the narrow, twisting road that hugged the side of the mountain, and on one sharp turn the rope broke, sending her suitcase along with squawking livestock thousands of feet to shatter on the rocks below. All her work was gone, along with any hope of starting again.

Betty told how after several of these major challenges to her faith, one day she climbed into her hammock and cried out to God: *Why am I even here?* she asked. She felt like a failure. *Don Macario—who was a certain answer to prayer—is dead; all my work is for nothing. I'm not even a good missionary. My work is worthless. I was going to bring the scriptures to these people! Now why am I here, and at such a great sacrifice?*

Betty told my mother that the Holy Spirit brought to her mind Isaiah 43:10:

> "You are my witnesses," says the LORD,
>> "and my servant whom I have chosen,
> that you may know and believe me
>> and understand that I am He."

God chose me to be his witness, she repeated again and again. *He wants me to know him.* Comforted, she realized that was all she needed to know. The "why" wasn't important. Just the knowledge that God is good and has a plan. In the end, she decided that she desired God above all else, not what she could do for him. She always spoke of that realization as a turning point in her life.

Years later, Elisabeth's second husband died of cancer. She married again, and on several occasions she talked with my mother about loss and seeking love and fulfillment. "Arlita," she said one day, "if I had all three husbands at one time, it wouldn't be enough!" She wasn't trying to put down her husbands—all three were wonderful men—but was making the point that there is no one person on earth who can ever fulfill us. In losing her work, she had learned to seek fulfillment not in achievement but in the Lord. In losing two husbands (and in loving three) she learned that only God can satisfy that longing for love we all have.

Elisabeth Elliot had a radio program for many years called *Gateway to Joy*.[3] My mother was her guest many times as they talked about the life of faith. Nearly every episode, Betty started by saying something from the Bible that I heard many times growing up: "I have loved you with an everlasting love" (Jer 31:3) . . . and "underneath are the everlasting arms" (Dt 33:27). In all of our searching, God—and only God—is where we can find what we long for.

GETTING THE CONTEXT

The theme of barrenness we saw in the story of Sarah is continued in the story of Isaac's wife, Rebekah, who had children only after twenty years of waiting. Then their son, Jacob, married Leah and Rachel, sisters who struggled in different ways with being barren or empty. One had Jacob's love but couldn't have his children; the other had plenty of children but never the love of her husband. Both were in anguish.

In the end, it was from those barren wombs and longing hearts that God birthed his Chosen People. Their emptiness points to a spiritual truth: everyone has a space inside them that is meant to be filled by God. As it says in the *Catechism*, "The desire for God is written in the human heart, because man is created by God and for God; and God never ceases to draw man to himself. Only in God will he find the truth and happiness he never stops searching for" (*CCC*, 27).

Most of us can relate to something in the story of Leah and Rachel. Each woman represents a different way to handle desire. There's a struggle either way—that's the fault of the Fall. But one path leads to comfort, fulfillment, strength, and life, while the other leads inevitably to tears and death.

God calls us out of the pain of our longing, not necessarily by erasing it or by giving us what we want but by giving us himself. His perfect love is always available; he's always there for us. As Caryll Houselander writes, "There is no escape from the invitation of the overflowing love that is God."[4]

Let's see what we can learn from Leah and Rachel.

LEAH AND RACHEL'S STORY

You can read about Leah and Rachel in Genesis 29–33.

LEAH ACHES FOR LOVE . . .

"Leah's eyes were weak, but Rachel was beautiful and lovely" (Gn 29:17).

Leah had weak eyes. Or maybe they were dull, or bleary, or even lovely—translators disagree on how to translate the word in this context. Let's give her the benefit of the doubt and say her eyes were lovely. Even then, she didn't have a chance beside her shapely, gorgeous little sister. The contrast must have been apparent to both, even without the benefit of mirrors. The way Rachel attracted approving glances everywhere she went. The way Leah wasn't noticed, or always came up short in comparison. I remember what it was like to be a shy and awkward junior when my cute, outgoing younger brother entered high school as a freshman. Within weeks

I was known as "Joe's sister." *But I came first!* I wanted to say. *It's not fair—notice me!* I love my brother, but I wasn't noticed when he was there. Was it like that for Leah?

One day, her father, Laban, brought home his nephew, Jacob. Jacob was the son of Isaac—promised son of Abraham and Sarah—and Rebekah, Laban's sister. They had sent him from Canaan to Laban's home up north to find a wife among his daughters. What a boon for Leah, who as the eldest should have married first! But Jacob had already met the lovely Rachel and had fallen hard. He offered to serve Laban for seven years for the hand of the younger sister.

Seven years should be plenty of time to find a spouse for Leah too, but as the time approached, Leah still was single. Rachel's wedding day arrived and Laban invited the guests and prepared a feast. All the men were drinking and celebrating, and eventually it was time to bring out the bride. Laban entered the girls' tent and said, *Leah, come with me.* Wait—Leah, not Rachel? *You're the oldest, you're going to marry Jacob.* We're not told what either girl thought about this deceitful move, but their silence suggests they were complicit. In fact, Jewish tradition honors Rachel for not begrudging her sister this opportunity to get married, thus allowing Leah to save face.[5]

Don't ask me how they pulled it off. I assume there was alcohol involved, and a veil, and probably no light in the tent. It's ironic that the weak-eyed sister pulled the wool over the eyes of a man who didn't see her. They consummated the marriage and in the morning, "Behold, it was Leah"! (Gn 29:25).

Wow. Jacob was furious. Laban offered to give him Rachel too, after Leah's wedding week, if only Jacob would work another seven years. The deal was made and a week later Jacob took Rachel as his second wife. "And he loved Rachel more than Leah. . . . Leah was hated" (Gn 29:30, 31).

Hated! That may not be as negative as it sounds. The Hebrew expression used in that verse is a legal term for "the unfavored co-wife."[6] But even if it only means that Jacob had no emotional attachment to Leah, think how devastating that would be for her. It's bad enough to have your husband love someone or something more than you, but to be caught up in that kind of a love triangle with your sister would be agony.

When the Lord saw the situation, he opened Leah's womb, but not Rachel's. And poor, unloved Leah began to bear sons for Jacob. Her heart bled out into their names:

Reuben means "see, a son": "Surely now my husband will love me" (Gn 29:32), she said.

Simeon means "the LORD has heard" that she's hated, thus "he has given me this son also" (Gn 29:33).

Levi means "joined": "Now this time my husband will be joined to me, because I have borne him three sons" (Gn 29:34).

Oh, the agony! Leah's longing for Jacob's love was so intense, she couldn't receive the blessing God gave her by those children. They were nothing more than means to the end she really wanted: the love of her husband. She was fertile, yet she felt barren. In Jacob's eyes, she was nothing but a baby mama, after all.

Leah suffered from the curse of the Fall: "In pain you shall bring forth children, yet your desire shall be for your husband" (Gn 3:16). How many women through the years have suffered that pain within their most intimate relationships? How many women have poured themselves out for someone, giving him all they have, giving him what he wants—only to be rejected, passed over, ignored? What is the answer?

Watch again how Leah named her sons (Gn 29:32–34):

- Reuben: "Surely now my husband will love me."
- Simeon: "Because the LORD has heard that I am hated, he has given me this son also."
- Levi: "Now this time my husband will be joined to me, because I have borne him three sons."

After her third child, Leah must have realized that she'd never get all she wanted from her husband. It's so tempting to think like that, that a man—this man, the right man—is all we need. *If only my husband loved me more,* we might say. Or, *If only I'd married this other one.* All the time not realizing that even with Mr. Right, the day will come when we'll wake up and realize he's not all that. The ache will still be there. Will we throw him over and find someone else to satisfy for a while, or will we realize that no one will ever be enough, as Elisabeth Elliot did, and look to the Lord?

. . . AND FINDS CONTENTMENT IN GOD

I believe Leah came to that realization. When she got pregnant a fourth time, something changed in her heart. Or maybe it was her eyes that changed. Instead of being "weak," they were focused intently on the Lord. She "conceived again and bore a son, and said, 'This time I will praise the LORD'; therefore she called his name Judah" (Gn 29:35). *Judah* means "praise."

What is it about praising God? In Psalm 63, the psalmist is thirsting in a land where there's no water. He can't find anything to slake his thirst, but he knows he can find it in God. He cries out, "Because your merciful love is better than life, my lips will praise you. So I will bless you as long as I live" (vv. 3–4). And it's in the praising that his "soul is feasted as with marrow and fat" (v. 5). Somehow it's true that when we take our minds off our problems and praise the Lord, we open our hearts to be filled.

Leah learned that lesson. From that point on, she was content with her growing family. Her maid bore two boys for her; she called one *Gad,* "Good fortune!" (Gn 30:11), and the other *Asher,* "Happy am I!" (Gn 30:13). Then when she had two more boys of her own, she saw that God had given her "a good dowry" (Gn 30:20) that would bring her honor from her husband. Her situation didn't change, but she did. Leah didn't find the love she looked for in marriage, but she found peace in what she had. At the end of her life, this unloved wife found honor when Jacob buried her with Sarah and Abraham and Isaac and Rebekah, in the place he asked to be buried too. She lay with Jacob in death while her sister, we will see, did not.

RACHEL CANNOT BE SATISFIED . . .

Poor Rachel.

For all her beauty and the devoted love of Jacob, she wasn't happy. There was a hole in her soul so wide, those things were nothing to her. And when Leah began to have children—four in a row to Rachel's none—it was more than she could take. The girl who all her life was valued over her older sister simply for her looks, who possibly pitied Leah, found herself lagging behind. Where Leah's inner beauty grew under pressure, Rachel's inner beauty began to sag. Rather than being grateful for what she had and trusting in God's goodness, Rachel envied Leah and begrudged her happiness. Envy doesn't just want something someone else has; it feels their success as a personal affront. In Rachel, envy spawned a stew of resentment that she dumped on Jacob: "Give me children, or I shall die!" (Gn 30:1) she said.

"I'm not God," he fired back in anger. "I can't make you have children" (see Genesis 30:2).

What was happening to their love? They played the blame game like Adam and Eve did after eating the forbidden fruit (Adam: "It's her fault." Eve: "The devil made me do it!" See Genesis 3:12–13). While my heart aches for Rachel's pain and infertility, what she did next shows that it wasn't children she wanted so much as to best her sister. Like Sarah before her, Rachel had her husband give her children through her maid. Here's what she named them:

Dan, meaning "he judged," as though having this child was her right: "God has judged me . . . and given me a son" (Gn 30:6).

Then Naphtali, which means "my wrestlings": "With mighty wrestlings I have wrestled with my sister, and have prevailed" (Gn 30:8).

It doesn't seem that Rachel cared about Jacob's love, or her sister, or the children. Having babies was a competition to her, not a joy. Rachel was all about Rachel.

Leah's maid bore two more sons for her, but she had stopped having children. When her son brought her some mandrakes (a plant root believed to have aphrodisiac powers), Rachel wanted some for herself. Leah refused—"Isn't it enough that you've taken my husband? Do you have to have everything?" (see Genesis 30:15). But when Rachel bartered a night with Jacob for the plants, Leah took her sister up on the offer. She went on to have two more sons and a daughter, while Rachel remained barren.

No amount of manipulating helped Rachel conceive. But at last, God opened her womb. "God has taken away my reproach," she said. So far, so good. But "she called his name Joseph, saying, 'May the LORD add to me another son!'" (Gn 30:23–24).

Rachel still wasn't satisfied. No sooner did she get what she wanted than she wanted another. She reminds me of Veruca Salt, the little rich girl in *Charlie and the Chocolate Factory* who always wants more. Or of Eve, who was given a garden full of delights but fixed her sights on the one tree she couldn't have. The vacuum in Rachel's heart sucked everything she got into a black hole where it disappeared into her longing.

Later in the story, Rachel stole her father's household gods. The Bible doesn't reveal her motive, but it seems that Jacob's God wasn't enough for her, just as Jacob's devotion wasn't enough and his child wasn't enough. That is the essence of idolatry. When things don't go our way, we're tempted to let go of trust in God and rely on ourselves or other things instead. Or when we fixate on something we want, we end up mentally "bowing down" to it. We may not have "household gods" in the shape of physical idols, but it's easy to make gods of marriage, sex, or babies (or riches, power, or things). But created things can never fill the need we have for God.

. . . BUT HER TEARS BEAR FRUIT

Rachel is a tragic figure. She went on to have a second son but died in childbirth (Gn 35:16–20). With her last breath, she named him *Ben-oni*, "son of my sorrow," but he's remembered by the name his father gave him: *Benjamin*, "son of the right hand." Jacob buried his beloved wife by the road to Ephrath.[7] Centuries later, the ten northern tribes of Israel (which by then were called by the name of Joseph's son) were taken captive by Assyria and marched away into exile from there. Jeremiah 31:15 links Rachel with that tragedy:

> Thus says the LORD:
> "A voice is heard in Ramah,
>   lamentation and bitter weeping.
> Rachel is weeping for her children;
>   she refuses to be comforted for her children,
>   because they are not."

It's not all bad, though. Her weeping will bear fruit. As that passage goes on to say, "There is hope for your future . . . and your children shall come back to their own country" (Jer 31:17). This is part of the messianic hope and expectation of the Jews.

Jewish tradition remembers Rachel for her tears and compassion—first in not begrudging Leah her husband in marriage, and then for praying for the exiles, many of whom actually descend from Leah. The rabbis say that Jacob buried her on the road and not in the family tomb because he foresaw that in generations to come, they would need her prayers.

A thousand years after Rachel and Leah married Jacob, people were still talking about them. When Ruth was married, the people pronounced this blessing: "May the LORD make [her] . . . like Rachel and Leah, who together built up the house of Israel" (Ru 4:11). Together these sisters built up Israel by having, between them and their handmaids, twelve sons who fathered the twelve tribes of Israel ("Israel" being another name for Jacob). Leah is responsible for two-thirds of the nation, and two of the tribes that come from her sons receive special honor: the Messiah comes from Judah, which is why Jesus is called the "lion of the tribe of Judah," and the priests come from Levi. So the woman who learned to stop expecting a man to fulfill her and who instead turned her eyes to her heavenly Father was specially blessed.

But good came from Rachel as well. Her firstborn, Joseph, is one of the finest men portrayed in the Old Testament (see Genesis 37–50). Sold by his brothers into slavery, Joseph rose to power in Egypt and saved his family from famine, reconciling his brothers to their father in the process and thus becoming a figure of Christ. He had a keen sense of God's ability to bring good out of a situation that someone else meant for harm (see Genesis 50:20). Joseph's brothers were jealous and vindictive, but he was a shining example of purity and faith in God. Did he learn some of that at his mother's knee? I wonder. Perhaps Rachel learned something from her experience after all.

CLAIMING LEAH AND RACHEL'S LEGACY: GOD ALONE IS ENOUGH

I find myself wondering why the author of Genesis took such care to describe the squabbles of this pair of rival sisters. Why not save a bit of ink and simply list the tribes that came from them, if that is their primary legacy? I think it's so we would know that God uses us as we are—struggles, insecurities, and all.

Hearing their story, we're drawn into their pain and identify with it, because we have desires too. And "you can't always get what you want," to quote the Rolling Stones. That's just a fact of life. And if you put all your focus on something you can't have, you risk being miserable and missing out on everything else as a result.

There was a time in my early twenties when I wanted to get married so badly, I didn't put much effort into other interests or even into following God. I had someone in mind, too, but nothing I did to get his attention seemed to work. I talked to Aunt Betty about it.

"Did he ask you to marry him?" she asked. "No? Well don't let that stop you from moving ahead!" She quoted something her first husband, Jim, had said: "Let not your longing slay the appetite of your living," which was exactly what I was doing. Having decided what I wanted, nothing else would do. I was miserable.

So I took her advice and moved on with my life.

Looking back now, having married a wonderful man and had children, good jobs, and many blessings, I see that as good as all these things have been, there's still a hole inside. I could be like Rachel, who took what she had for granted, and try to find more fulfillment somewhere else. Or I can be like Leah, be grateful for my blessings and set my eyes on God. The problem is, when we don't look to God to fulfill us, no matter what we find to put in it, the hole in our heart remains. And instead of feeling that hole as *capacity*, like a nest ready to receive life, we feel it as *emptiness*.

The seventeenth-century French philosopher Blaise Pascal wrote of an "infinite abyss" inside every person that we try and try to fill but that can only be filled by God (see *Pensées* VII, 425).[8] That concept entered the popular imagination as a "God-shaped vacuum" in our souls. I love that description. It makes me think of the black holes of powerful gravity that exist in the universe. That's what each of us is like inside without God: a black hole that sucks things in but is never filled. The earth was like that before creation. But God spoke his Word into that black hole, said "let there be light," and the light banished the darkness. He spoke again and the world took shape, and it was good.

What God did with the universe, he wants to do with you. He loves you. And he wants to fill that sucking void—that vacuum in your heart—by sending his Word (his Son) to fill you with goodness, beauty, and purpose.

The story of Leah and Rachel shows that he can. These two very real, imperfect women, who lived in a tangle of heartbreak and domestic unrest, became the mothers and matriarchs of the twelve tribes of Israel. God's love provided comfort in heartbreak, turned emptiness into capacity. It makes me wonder, when I struggle with my own empty heart, if I say yes and receive him, might the Lord do something extraordinary with me?

QUESTIONS FOR REFLECTION

- What in Elisabeth's experience, or the story of Rachel or Leah, resonates with you? How have you experienced something similar?
- How have you experienced that "God-shaped vacuum"? When have you felt an ache in your heart that nothing has been able to fill?
- What did you learn from this chapter that might help you find contentment?

MIRIAM

GOD'S LOVE GIVES US WORTH

For I brought you up from the land of Egypt,
 and redeemed you from the house of
 bondage;
and I sent before you Moses,
 Aaron, and Miriam.

—Micah 6:4

Such holy women as . . . Miriam . . . kept alive
the hope of Israel's salvation.
 —*Catechism of the Catholic Church*, 64

"Now—let—us—sing!"

A chorus of voices filled the living room. There were probably thirty of us, adults sitting on couches and chairs, and kids sprawled on the floor and in their parents' laps. We sang for a full hour, one worship song after another. Most were based on scripture.

"Psalm 100!" someone called. My mother struck a note on the autoharp and we all started in. "Make a joyful / noise unto the LORD, / all ye lands!"

My mother started the "sings" in our house when I was in high school. The nondenominational church they had been going to, which was known for its music and praise-filled worship, had collapsed. Mourning that loss and longing for a way to restore the fellowship they missed, my parents began inviting friends over on Sunday afternoons. The first time, people stayed so long we all ended up sitting around the kitchen table with cereal and bananas.

After that, everyone brought food and we ate potluck. An hour of singing, then food, and then whoever could would stay on and pray while the kids played. Sometimes it went on into the night. Anywhere from a dozen friends to six times that or more would come. For twenty years my parents had those sings, first weekly and later monthly or by invitation. They stopped only when Mother's cancer kept her from hosting them.

There was power in those gatherings—power in the prayer but also power in the singing. There's something about lifting your voice to God, especially in the words of the Psalms. If you have something to be thankful for, it gives shape to your gratefulness. And if you don't, the song becomes a place into which to pour your overflowing heart. The psalms give voice to your sorrow and pain, and singing them lifts up your heart. It resets your focus on God and gives you hope.

One thing I always remember from those days is Mother's autoharp. You don't have to be a trained musician to play one, you just push the button that has the key you want, and start to strum. She'd put it on her lap and push the buttons while kids took turns on the strings. Or she'd lift it up and hold it close to her chest and do the strumming herself, setting the beat and filling the room with joy. It was a simple, ordinary thing that contributed to extraordinary worship.

That was in the '70s, a time when lots of Christians got interested in their Jewish heritage and started singing songs with an Israeli flavor. When we sang those at the sings, Mom or one of her friends would get out a tambourine and some of us would dance. One of our favorites was the song Miriam sang by the Red Sea: "I will sing unto the Lord, for he has triumphed gloriously; the horse and rider thrown into the sea!" (Ex 15:1). We sang our hearts out, imagining we were with the children of Israel that day.

I saw one of my friends from those days recently. It's been years since we last met, but the time dissolved as we reminisced. That worship helped form both of us. It strengthened us in faith. We saw how it took our parents through hard times and we gravitate toward it as adults, *knowing* the power of praise. Both of us hope we've passed it on to our own children. I was never bold enough to shake a tambourine, but now I'm thinking . . . maybe I can get an autoharp and teach my grandkids.

GETTING THE CONTEXT

Four hundred years after Rachel and Leah fought to build the family of Jacob, their twelve sons with their families have moved to Egypt. They were blessed and multiplied, but they were living on borrowed real estate. Somewhere along the way, one of the kings of Egypt became nervous by the sheer numbers of these immigrants. He decided to oppress them and make them his slaves.

The story of their liberation is dominated by Moses. Yet God used women, too, to birth his new nation. Without the courageous assistance of Moses's mother, Jochebed; his sister, Miriam; the Pharaoh's daughter; and Moses's wife, Zipporah, Moses would not have lived to save his people. These women were Hebrew, Egyptian, and Midianite; they were old and young and middle-aged; they were rich and they were poor. All of them were strong, with courage born of faith.

The woman who emerges most clearly from the biblical story—and who we will get to know in this chapter—is Miriam. She was the older sister of Moses and Aaron, and together the three of them led the children of Israel out of slavery and through the desert to the Promised Land. Like Moses, she is remembered as a prophet.[1] It was the prophet Micah who put her on par with her more famous brothers when he wrote that God said of Israel,

> For I brought you up from the land of Egypt,
>   and redeemed you from the house of bondage;
> and I sent before you Moses,
>   Aaron, and Miriam. (Mi 6:4)

We should not be surprised that God continues to use both men and women to launch the nation of Israel, just as he started humanity with Adam and Eve and then called Abram and Sarai to make a new start. Miriam's role in the Exodus is as essential as it is uniquely feminine. As Pope John Paul II writes in his *Letter to Women*, "Women are ever ready and willing to give themselves generously to others, especially in serving the weakest and most defenseless. In this work they exhibit a kind of *affective, cultural and spiritual motherhood* which has inestimable value for the development of individuals and the future of society."[2]

Spiritual motherhood shines through Miriam, even from a very young age. She played a critical role in building Israel. Even though she made mistakes, she is a model for all of us.

MIRIAM'S STORY

You can read about Miriam in Exodus 2:1–10; Exodus 15:1–21; Numbers 12:1–15; and Numbers 20:1–2.

The Hebrew name *Miriam* (or *Miryam*; in Greek or Latin, *Mary* or *Maria*) comes from words meaning "bitterness" and "rebellion." The name fits her. Miriam was born into the bitterness of slavery in Egypt and in her actions she rebelled in a good way against the dictates of evil and in a wrong way against her brother's God-given authority. Scripture gives us four snapshots of Miriam, at four very different times in her life, that reveal her complex character.

SNAPSHOT 1: MIRIAM SAVES HER BROTHER (EX 2:7–8)

Tall, willowy reeds form a lush fringe along the Nile, providing shelter and privacy. A woman bends among the reeds and tucks a little basket among them. Her face is a study in anguished prayer: cradled in the basket is her son, just three months old. He (with all other newborn Hebrew males) has been condemned by Pharaoh to be cast to his death in the river. Jochebed, the mother, is so focused on her painful task that even as she leaves, she doesn't see that her young daughter has followed her. The girl stands at a distance, watching to see what will become of the boy. A ways off, and on her way to bathe in the Nile, is Pharaoh's daughter with her maid.

The little girl in the picture is Miriam, even though she isn't named. Her baby brother is Moses. Their parents, Jochebed and Amram, were God-fearing, faithful people. According to Jewish tradition, Amram prayed fervently that God would save his people from slavery.[3] God answered him in a dream, promising that his newborn son would one day deliver Israel from slavery. So he and Jochebed hid Moses "by faith" because "they were not afraid of the king's edict" (Heb 11:23).

Young Miriam must have helped to care for Moses. Children love babies, and little girls so often want to mother them! Surely she helped quiet him during those first three months. Jochebed must have told her daughter why she was weaving the basket for Moses. By setting the baby afloat on the Nile instead of tossing him defenseless into the water, the mother was obeying the king's edict while putting Moses into the hands of God. I'm sure that Jochebed's faith in a God who is greater than Pharaoh helped to form Miriam's convictions. How else could she have done what she did next?

When Pharaoh's daughter discovered the baby, Miriam leaped into action. The princess looked on him with pity, knowing he was destined to die. Would she follow Pharaoh's edict, take him from the basket, and leave him to drown? Miriam didn't give her a chance to carry out the fatal order. Instead, she offered to find a nurse from among the Hebrew women. "Go," the princess simply said, and Miriam ran off to get Jochebed. Here's another woman, Egyptian this time, who valued life. Whether it was her idea first or Miriam's, she defied Pharaoh's order and adopted the boy, paying Jochebed to nurse and raise him.

Who was Miriam? From this one scene in her early life we can see she was brave with the faith of her parents. Her leadership qualities shone. Through her quick-thinking speech and action, Moses was not only saved from a watery grave but also restored to his mother. Young Miriam stood over the little basket that might have carried her brother to his death and wept in her heart, yearning for a way to save him and acting on a chance that came by. She is a model for us of caring for the vulnerable and daring to challenge evil even when we are weak ourselves.

SNAPSHOT 2: MIRIAM LEADS BY THE RED SEA (EX 15:1, 20–21)

Our next snapshot of Miriam is taken by water as well, this time the Red Sea. Eighty years had passed before Moses's sister is mentioned again. Eighty years,[4] while Moses grew up in the Egyptian court and then went into exile after killing an Egyptian who abused a Hebrew slave. Only after Pharaoh died did God call Moses to return and deliver his people.

And now it has happened. Freedom! The people are standing on the far shore of the sea, breathless from a long ordeal. They have endured not only generations of bitter slavery but also the awe-inspiring plagues God had sent upon the Egyptians—including the horror of Egyptian cries when the angel of death, who had "passed over" the Hebrews, had slain the Egyptians' firstborn sons. Finally, they had made their improbable escape between great walls of water. And as those walls crashed down upon their enemy, who was in hot pursuit behind them, the Israelites turned, safe upon the shore, and beheld the marooned chariots and dead bodies that littered the shore. Now the Israelites, with Moses, are singing praise to God. And the women are dancing!

Scripture says that Miriam, "the prophetess, the sister of Aaron, took a timbrel in her hand; and all the women went out after her with timbrels and dancing. And Miriam sang to them: 'Sing to the Lord, for he has triumphed gloriously; the horse and his rider he has thrown into the sea'" (Ex 15:20–21). What a way to take their minds off their troubles and get them ready to move on!

The little girl who acted on her parents' faith had become a leader. The ancient rabbis taught that just as God sent Moses before Israel to teach God's Word and Aaron to make atonement, he sent Miriam to teach the women (*Targum Micha* 6:4). Miriam also had become a prophetess in her own right. By the shore of the Red Sea, she led the women in God-inspired praise.

What a celebration that must have been!

Stop a minute and think of what had to happen first to make that possible. Women who had been slaves all their lives—who were born into slavery, whose mothers and grandmothers were slaves—had timbrels (tambourines) with them and they knew how to dance.

Life was brutal in Egypt. Just keeping their families together must have taken all that they had. Yet these women made instruments and learned how to play them! And that final night (see Exodus 12), when they were getting ready to leave so quickly that there wasn't time for bread to rise, as their neighbors wailed over the loss of their firstborn sons, *they packed their tambourines.*

"Sing to the Lord!" Miriam sang. And all the women followed her, dancing and singing and playing their timbrels in a kind of antiphonal refrain.

For years, Miriam must have worked to keep the flame of hope alive, that one day God would free them. The other women as well: Jewish tradition speaks of the faith of the Hebrew women who prepared instruments while they were still slaves, refusing to give up hope. The *Catechism*, too, counts Miriam among women who "kept alive the hope of Israel's salvation" (64).

Miriam taught the women to make instruments and sing and praise God in advance for a deliverance that lived only in their hearts. She led with "a feminine strength born out of bitterness," writes Chana Weisberg. "Mourning their murdered children with their feminine sensitivity . . . , the women found the strength to fortify themselves not to lose hope. . . . Amidst their agony, the women prepared tambourines. They fanned the spark of yearning within their worn souls until it grew into an overpowering, inextinguishable flame of faith."[5]

Looking back on this event in the light of Christ, St. Ambrose saw Miriam as a type of the Church leading the redeemed in songs of praise.[6] This worship is the "work" of the people. *Work* and *worship* are the same word in Hebrew: *avad*. And Exodus contrasts the back-breaking, life-sucking *avad* required by Pharaoh with the jubilant, life-giving *avad* required by God. The people were set free from Pharaoh's work *in order to worship God*. It was no accident that worship was the first thing they did after getting across the Red Sea. They may have been exhausted and emotionally spent, but Miriam was there, ready with her instrument to lift them—body, soul, and spirit—into the presence of God. "[The Lord is] enthroned on the praises of Israel," says Psalm 22:3. Miriam helped them get to the throne room.

SNAPSHOT 3: MIRIAM CRITICIZES IN THE DESERT (NM 12:1–15)

The next thread of Miriam's story emerges in the wilderness, about a year after the Red Sea crossing. There's not a drop of water in sight, and that dry place forms a fitting backdrop for an episode in which Miriam spoke against Moses and was punished. Instead of using her position to give life and point others toward God, she did the opposite. This scene highlights her humanity and serves as a warning to us.

As the scene opens, there's been trouble in the camp. God has been traveling with the Israelites, protecting them and providing miraculous food, but their constant complaining has wearied Moses and angered God. Already fire has broken out around the camp and plague has killed off many of the complainers. On the flip side, God has helped Moses by putting some of his spirit on seventy men who will be able to bear some of the burden of leadership. But Miriam and Aaron, who should have been at Moses's right hand, have spoken against him.

Their complaint was triggered by something to do with the Cushite woman Moses married. But there was more to it than that: "Has the LORD indeed only spoken through Moses?" they asked. "Has he not spoken through us also?" (Nm 12:2). Miriam and Aaron must have felt their younger brother was getting too big for his britches, or that their voices were getting lost. Suddenly God's voice rang out: "You three. In my office, now" (see Numbers 12:4).

Well, maybe not his office, but to what amounted to the same thing—the "tent of meeting" where God lived among his people and where he met with Moses and spoke to him. God summoned the three siblings he had sent before his people. Then from a pillar of cloud, he chastised Miriam and Aaron. "Listen to me," he said. "I speak to prophets in dreams, but I speak to Moses face-to-face. I entrusted him with my whole house (all Israel). How is it that you weren't afraid to speak against him?" (see Numbers 12:6–8).

When the cloud lifted, Miriam's skin was leprous. She, the oldest, was likely the instigator. Aaron rushed to her defense, begging Moses not to punish her for their offense. Then Moses cried out to God to heal her. He evidently did, but still she had to spend seven days shut up outside of the camp. Perhaps out of respect for her, no one moved on until she was brought back in.

I find myself wanting to defend Miriam. Her punishment seems harsh, her complaint justifiable. She must have known Moses as well as (if not better than) anyone—"warts and all," as they say. She saved him as a baby, probably helped raise him. She must have known the shyness and fear that made him shrink from God's call and lean on Aaron as spokesperson. As they set out through the desert, she must have seen how Moses buckled under the pressure of complaints and said he'd rather die, blaming God for giving the burden to him alone (Nm 11:11–15).

That's when God gave a prophetic spirit to seventy elders, to help strengthen Moses. And it was soon after that that Miriam and Aaron spoke against him. I can't say I blame them. Miriam was a prophetess. Did she and Aaron feel as though they were being replaced? Why didn't Moses lean on them for support? And from

Miriam's point of view, why would Moses feel he needed to carry the people "in [his] bosom," like a nursing mother (as he said in Numbers 11:12)? Wasn't she there beside her brother to do the more "motherly" tasks?

Scripture doesn't comment on any of this. There's just an acknowledgment, on Aaron's part, that he and Miriam have foolishly sinned. What was the sin? It doesn't seem to have to do with the content of their complaint as much as the fact of it. I'm tempted to shout, *Wait! She might have a point! Moses looks weak—why not rely more on Miriam?* But it wasn't about gifting or ability. God entrusted Moses, and him only, to be a kind of prime minister, responsible for the nation. Miriam may have been sent by God as a leader along with her brothers, but it wasn't up to her to pass judgment on God's chief appointee or to decide who was worthy of being a prophet.

Maybe more to the point, Miriam was a respected leader and she spoke her judgment out loud. To publicly cast doubt on God's appointed authority was a dangerous thing to do in a charged atmosphere of discontent. The people already were challenging Moses and doubting God's care. They had just finished burying a whole lot of people who complained. Miriam's critique could have reignited the whole issue.

"So the tongue is a little member and boasts of great things," writes St. James. "How great a forest is set ablaze by a small fire!" (Jas 3:5). His words echo the book of Proverbs: "Death and life are in the power of the tongue" (Prv 18:21), and "rash words are like sword thrusts, but the tongue of the wise brings healing" (Prv 12:18).

I think of how often I've spoken, with a "good" motive, against someone: to set the record straight, to justify myself, or because someone "needs to know." When those words cut someone else, it's so hard to take them back! Just because something is true doesn't mean it must be said. Yet the right words at the right time can do good. As St. Paul said, "Let no evil talk come out of your mouths, but only such as is good for edifying, as fits the occasion, that it may impart grace to those who hear" (Eph 4:29). Words can give grace!

Just think of Miriam's example: her words, wrongly spoken, may have brought leprosy and isolation on herself in the desert. But her words also saved Moses and reunited him with his mother. And her song led weary people in praise of God by the shore of the Red Sea.

SNAPSHOT 4: MIRIAM REMEMBERED AT HER DEATH (NM 20:1–2)

In this final frame, Miriam has died and been buried. There's not much to the image, especially if you compare it to what we learn about the deaths of Moses and Aaron. But Hebrew commentary from ancient times has read Miriam's death in context of what came next: immediately after she died, there was no water and the congregation revolted against Moses and Aaron.

What is the significance of this? Due to the association of Miriam with water and redemption in other accounts of her life, Jewish tradition credits Miriam with being a spiritual oasis in the desert—a source of life and healing for the people. According to the Midrash (ancient commentary on the scriptures), God provided a miraculous well of living water in the desert as long as she lived. As it says in the Talmud, "Three great leaders led Israel: Moses, Aaron, and Miriam. In their merit they received three great gifts: the Well [Miriam], the Clouds of Glory [Aaron], and the Manna [Moses]" (*Ta'anit* 9a).

Because of this, while the biblical account of Miriam's death seems to slight her, the Jewish people continue to hold her in high esteem. The first-century historian Josephus, for example, in his history of the Jews, describes an elaborate burial and a mourning period for Miriam equal to that of her brothers.[7] More recently, in his commentary on Numbers 19:1–22:1, Rabbi Ed Rosenthal writes that "the greatness of Miriam was that she was the embodiment of the honor and glory of the women of Israel."[8]

CLAIMING MIRIAM'S LEGACY: GOD USES US DESPITE OUR IMPERFECTIONS

As I look back over Miriam's life, I'm grateful for these very different snapshots of her character. She's not perfect, and who of us is? I can see it going through my own photo albums. There are times when I was at the top of my game, and it shows. Those are the pages I'm proud to let people see. But then there are the pictures I don't like to look at.

There's one my brother took when we were kids; we were in a canoe and I turned around to yell at him. Man, could I be bossy! The expression on my face is ugly. I'm not sure why that picture made it into the album, and now the glue on those transparent pages is stuck so hard I'd have to take the whole page out and lose both front and back. So it stays, reminding me that whatever I'd like to think about myself, I'm not always nice, that I must be careful how I treat people.

Then there are the albums in the back of the cupboard, the ones I haven't made a point to show the kids. Those hold the stories I don't tell, they companion the journals I plan to burn before I die. And if I do, what will be left for posterity but the carefully curated Facebook entries, the pretty Instagram shots? Everything lovely and nicely arranged.

If Moses or anyone else who wrote the Bible were around today, I don't think much of it would end up on social media. It's too raw. People show all their warts, like Miriam in the desert. Like Rachel fighting with her sister, Leah crying over her unloving husband. Like Sarah persecuting Hagar. The men too: Abraham's weakness, Moses's anger, King David's lust and murder . . . (see 2 Samuel 11). Nobody's perfect. They all fail. Yet they are examples God has given us of faith.

There is hope in this for us! We can learn from these spiritual mothers as Miriam learned from her mother, and pass on what we learn. That's what spiritual motherhood is all about. Even young children can live by faith, and faith can strengthen them. What sustained Miriam through eighty years of slavery while Moses was being raised in the Egyptian court, then living in exile, and finally preparing to lead the people out of Egypt? Her faith, the faith she got from her parents, sustained her. And at the end of her life, even given her lapse, she was buried with honor and still is remembered with honor.

God doesn't value or love us based on our worth, measured according to some impossible standard of perfection. On the contrary, we are worth a great deal *because he loves us.*

My favorite snapshot from Miriam's album will always be the one taken beside the Red Sea. After generations of slavery, God's family needed to learn that life with him isn't about work, but worship. They needed to worship God even before they found water, food, or even rest. Israel was to be a people of faith, as we learned from Sarah and Abraham. Miriam, with her timbrel, song, and dance, led them like a mother spoon-feeding her babies.

As I head into another week of work, I hope to remember Miriam, to take along my tambourine, so to speak (or learn to play the autoharp!), even if I'm overwhelmed. I want to watch for opportunities to lift up others, to be careful how I use my words. And even when life is bitter or I feel as if I'm about to drown, I will *prepare* to praise.

QUESTIONS FOR REFLECTION

- What in the opening story or Miriam's life resonates with you? How have you experienced something similar?
- In what particular way is God calling you to speak in strength, or lead in praise, or reconsider certain words?
- Consider the Miriams in your life, particularly those who were once a kind of oasis but have passed out of your life. What is their legacy to you?

- What did you learn from Miriam that might strengthen your faith or help you to praise?

RAHAB

GOD IS IN CONTROL OF THE STORMS OF OUR LIVES

> By faith Rahab the harlot did not perish with those who were disobedient, because she had given friendly welcome to the spies.
> —Hebrews 11:31

During the Communist takeover of China in 1949, my mother's parents were Christian missionaries in Shanghai. They had five young children and were expecting another. Mother remembers huddling with her family in the living room behind the blackout curtains, hearing bombs falling all around them. They listened daily to the radio reports as the Communist forces marched toward Shanghai. Then, in the middle of the confusion and threats, a great typhoon hit, putting the attacks on hold. Neither the Communists nor the Nationalists could do anything for days.

Mom tells how her mother, hearing the wind howling in the streets and the rain lashing the windows, ran to the door and flung it open. Her face was radiant with joy. "This is my God's storm!" she cried. Grandma Helen knew who was in control—of the storm and of the war. Others might put their trust in one of the political parties, but she knew they were in the hands of the God who rules the universe and yet loves each one of us. She knew that God is good . . . all the time, whatever the circumstances.

Grandma Helen knew that from experience. Eight years earlier, they were missionaries in Sumatra when the Japanese bombed Pearl Harbor and prepared to invade Sumatra. The family had to flee for their lives. Against terrible odds they made it onto the last ship out, the USS *President Madison*. They set off into the sea, dodging mines and submarines, not knowing if they'd ever make it home. Every day they heard of other ships that had been sunk. Some ships sank as they watched. Over and over they sang a hymn: "Jesus is a wonderful Savior, He will carry you through." Three months later, an astonished New York received them with the headline, "Ghost Ship Arrives!"

God had carried them through, indeed.

Long after she was grown and had children of her own, my mother met a woman from another family, employed by Shell oil company, that had tried to escape but missed that ship by just two hours. They were captured by the Japanese and put in prison camps. The woman was only nine at the time. Like my mother, she had survived, but only through a crucible.

Two families, both praying for God's help in a tremendous storm. One escaped, the other didn't. What does that say about God, faith, and hope? Grandma used to say, "Our really frightening stories are all about what didn't happen to us!" But if the worst had come to pass, she always added, she still would trust. God always can bring a greater good out of a bad situation, even a terribly evil one. In everything he works for good for those who love him (see Romans 8:28). As the Lord assured the Christian mystic Julian of Norwich in the turmoil of fourteenth-century England, we must hold steadfast to the faith and earnestly believe that "all manner of thing shall be well."[1]

I've been blessed to live in relatively peaceful times, but with the way things are going today, it's easy to fear that war might come here too. Storms come on the personal level as well. Who hasn't faced a time when the world seemed to be falling apart? A loved one dies or loses a job, or some disaster hits the family. I've had times when several things have hit at once—wave upon wave, with no end in sight!

Who is in control of the storms of our lives? And where can we go for help? It's times like these that I think of my grandmother's faith. She practiced it in the day-to-day, and it held her steady when times got rough. What I wouldn't give to have her faith and joy!

I'm reminded again of St. Paul's confidence that the faith that first lived in Timothy's grandmother and mother also lives in him (2 Tm 1:4–5). But it wasn't enough that they had passed him their faith. Timothy had to own it. Paul charged him to rekindle the gift of God he had received and to live courageously in the power God provides (2 Tm 1:6–8). Like Timothy, I can't ride on anyone's coattails. It's up to me to act on what I know and have been given. Thank God, he's the same God, and he's in charge of my storms too.

GETTING THE CONTEXT

At the start of the book of Joshua, the storm of war was about to hit Canaan.

Forty years before, the Canaanites had heard how Israel's God dried up the Red Sea and delivered the people from Egypt. More recently, and closer to home, they heard how Israel, with God's help, destroyed two Amorite kings. And now the people of Israel are lined up on the shore across the Jordan, getting ready to come in. The Canaanites are scared to death.

Standing just north of the Dead Sea and about five miles west of the Jordan River, the city of Jericho is heavily fortified. The archeological remains show a massive, 4.5-feet-thick defensive wall strengthened with rectangular stone towers. There would have been a second wall inside the first, with houses set in between them. Jericho would take the brunt of Israel's attack when it entered the land.

The Bible tells us what happened from the viewpoint of Israel, but at the same time, it gives us a glimpse of the people who live in Jericho. We see them through the story of a woman named Rahab.

Like Abraham and Sarah, Rahab left the many gods of her ancestors to follow the one true God, and she became one of just two women named in the Hebrews 11 "hall of faith."

The strength of Rahab's faith is especially remarkable when you consider her origins: Rahab was a Canaanite. Unlike Timothy, she didn't have the advantage of a grandmother Eunice or mother Lois from whom to draw her faith in Yahweh. Rahab's faith was built solely on what she heard about Israel's God . . . and when the storm came, she staked her life on it.

RAHAB'S STORY

You can read about Rahab in Joshua 2–6.

Rahab isn't your typical Old Testament heroine. She was a prostitute who ran an inn on the edge of the city of Jericho. Her house was built into the wall and looked out over the mountains to the west. When Joshua sent a couple of spies in ahead of his armies, they slipped into town and sought lodging with her.

Perhaps they thought no one would notice them in that part of town; but news spread of the visitors and the king ordered Rahab to give them up. But she had already hidden them on the roof, under stalks of flax she had set out to dry, and she told the king's officials they had gone. "Run and you can probably catch them!" she said, and they took off toward the Jordan River, where they assumed the spies were headed, and the gates of Jericho closed tightly after them (see Joshua 2:5).

Already we can see that Rahab thought for herself. She was independent and courageous—two characteristics that may have come in handy for someone living on the margins of society. And by harboring the spies, she defied the king's authority.

Rahab was perceptive. The spies may have looked defenseless, all locked up in a city that wanted them dead, but Rahab believed their side would win! Rahab was someone who could step back from the immediate situation and see a bigger picture.

RAHAB'S BARGAIN

When the king's men were gone and the spies were out of danger at least for a time, Rahab hurried up to the roof and made a bargain with them: "You promise to save my life and my family, and I will save you," she said (see Joshua 2:12–13). In the process, she gave the spies the intel they came for. Here's what she told them:

> I know that the LORD has given you the land, and that the fear of you has fallen upon us, and that all the inhabitants of the land melt away before you. For we have heard how the LORD dried up the water of the Red Sea before you when you came out of Egypt, and what you did to the two kings of the Amorites . . . whom you utterly destroyed. And as soon as we heard it, our hearts melted, and there was no courage left in any man, because of you; for the LORD your God is he who is God in heaven above and on earth beneath. (Jos 2:9–11)

Talk about good news! Forty years after God freed Israel from Egypt, the Canaanites' fear of God was so great, they were still in a panic! So why wasn't Rahab cringing in fright? Why didn't she turn in the spies? What made her different from everyone else?

Rahab's independent thinking helped her. Everyone in the land was staring the same facts straight in the face:

- They knew who God is. ("The LORD your God is he who is God in heaven above and on earth beneath" [Jos 2:11].)
- They knew what God had done, and therefore how powerful he is. ("The LORD dried up the water of the Red Sea before you when you came out of Egypt," and you "utterly destroyed" the Amorite kings [Jos 2:10].)
- They knew what God had promised. ("I know that the LORD has given you the land" [Jos 2:9].)

Out of everyone in Canaan, only Rahab chose to look at those things and trust in that God. The others only feared.

RAHAB'S FAITH IS BASED ON TRUTH . . .

Rahab reminds us that faith isn't based on feelings; it's not a blind leap into the dark. Her faith prompted her to act upon a knowledge of truth. The *Catechism* tells us that "faith is first of all a personal adherence of man to God. At the same time, . . . it is a *free assent to the whole truth that God has revealed*" (*CCC*, 150; emphasis in the original). That describes Rahab. Her faith in God, based on what she had learned about him, gave her courage to hide the spies, protect them from the soldiers, and put her hope for survival in the God of Israel.

As the spies settled on the roof, Rahab cut a deal with them. "Now then," she said, "swear to me by the LORD that as I have dealt kindly with you, you also will deal kindly with my father's house" (Jos 2:12).

Rahab was savvy. She pledged to save their lives if they would save hers and her family's. Was she just saving her skin? Bargaining for a chance at life? Perhaps—but isn't that what we all want from God, to overcome evil, death, and suffering? Knowing that God is all-powerful and that he has made a promise made Rahab follow God, not fight him. It was really the only reasonable response.

. . . AND COMPLETED IN WORKS

In the New Testament, James uses Rahab's story to explain why faith is more than just believing something is true: "Was not also Rahab the harlot also justified by works [and not only by faith] when she received the messengers and sent them out by another way? For as a body apart from the spirit is dead, so faith apart from works is dead" (Jas 2:25–26).

James is saying that it's not enough to have faith—mere belief—by itself. After all, everyone in Canaan believed God was the power behind Israel. And as James points out, even the demons believe God, and they tremble! (Jas 2:19). Rahab didn't just know things about God and believe them; she acted upon them. She staked her life on those things, in fact. Rahab's faith set her apart because she put it into action.

The devil would love us to think we have faith simply because we hold in our minds a set of truths. But Pope Benedict warns against "practical" atheism[2]—that is, *saying* we believe in God while at the same time *living* as though God doesn't exist. How many of us do that? How often are we in trouble—maybe we can't pay the bills, a child is sick, or a spouse is unfaithful—and we focus so hard on the crisis that we lose faith in the God who is able to help, or we forget that he cares enough to be with us? How often are we tempted not to give money or food to someone who needs it because we want to be sure our own family has enough? Do we doubt that God will provide?

How often do we fail to bear witness to the truth because we're not sure how it will be received? How often, when someone criticizes the Church or the Catholic faith, have we been afraid to speak up? When push comes to shove, will we stand on the promises of God and act on them?

We call ourselves Catholic, go faithfully to Mass, send our kids to religious education classes or Catholic school. We go to Bible study, serve as communion ministers . . . and then on Monday we go out into the world. Does it all go out the window?

"Faith . . . is an encounter with God who speaks and works in history and converts our daily life, transforming within us mentalities, value judgments, decisions and practical actions," Pope Benedict said.[3] He could have been describing Rahab. She was a woman whose life was transformed by what she learned about God. She staked her life on what she knew to be true about him, and on that basis she had hope for her future.

So . . . we might as well ask, did her faith pan out?

RAHAB'S FAITH GAVE HER HOPE

Before Rahab let the spies escape through her window, she asked them for "a sure sign" (Jos 2:12) that they would save her life in return. She wanted a pledge, something tangible.

"Swear to me," said Rahab. "Give me a sure sign" (Jos 2:12). She wanted something she could really depend on. They swore to her, and they told her to "bind this scarlet cord in the window" (Jos 2:18) and when they destroyed Jericho, everyone in her house would be saved. The scarlet cord was the sure sign.

Why scarlet? It reminds me of the blood the Israelites had to paint over their doors in Egypt so the angel of death would pass over them. Rahab had to publicly proclaim her allegiance, it seems, to be saved. And why a cord? *Cord* in Hebrew is *tikvah*—it's a string or rope of several strands twisted together for strength. The word also means "to look for," "to wait with patience," "to hope."

Most of the times *tikvah* is used in the Old Testament, it's in the book of Job. His situation seems completely hopeless, yet he has hope (*tikvah*) in God.

When Rahab asked the spies for a "sure sign," they told her to bind a scarlet cord—a scarlet hope—in the window. That scarlet cord was a pledge of her salvation like the blood of the Passover lambs was for Israel and like the blood of Jesus is for us. It was not a wish or a longing but rather a certain hope, full of expectation that she would obtain what was promised. And "hope does not disappoint," as St. Paul writes in Romans 5:5. He also writes that "hope that is seen is not hope. For who hopes for what he sees?" (Rom 8:24). By definition, hope involves waiting.

Rahab had to wait for days.

Imagine what those days were like for her and her family. The city gates were barred and the people of Jericho waited inside in fear, wondering when the Israelites would come and what they would do. Then one morning the Jordan River backed up in a heap about sixteen miles north of Jericho. Israel's priests carried the ark of the covenant, which was the seat of God's presence, into the riverbed. Then they stood there while all of the people walked across on dry land. It was like the Red Sea crossing all over again. Joshua 5:1 says that when the kings of Canaan heard what happened, their hearts melted "and there was no longer any spirit in them."

No one went in or out of Jericho. They waited in fear, while Rahab waited in hope.

Israel began a daily march around the city walls. There was no sound but the eerie trumpeting of rams' horns. Imagine Rahab peering out her window, telling her family not to be afraid, checking each day to make sure that scarlet cord was in place.

I have to wonder—did any of the townspeople see that cord? What did they think it was? Did they ask her? Did her neighbors worry it would draw attention to their homes? The Bible doesn't tell us, but we know it wasn't subtle. It had to stand out like a red flag for the invading army to notice it.

That says to me that true faith isn't private. It's visible to others. Lots of people today would argue with that. They'd say that faith is something that exists in a person's mind, that it should stay where it is and not affect decisions, actions, or behavior that can be seen in public.

But faith like that is dead.

Sometimes our faith makes us stand out in ways that make us uncomfortable. We're afraid we'll look different. It might make others angry or fearful, or make them ridicule us or even hate us. But faith that doesn't show on the outside can't save us. It's not a living faith.

The scarlet cord gave Rahab hope. It was her assurance that she would be saved. I wonder if it gave the Israelite army hope as well. They undoubtedly saw it every day as they circled the walls. Red stands out like neon against sandstone in the desert. Was the army afraid? Did they feel silly just marching around, day after day, doing nothing? Maybe the sight of that scarlet cord gave Israel evidence of something they couldn't see: it was a sure sign of the outsider Rahab's faith that Israel's God was stronger than the Canaanite gods. It was a reminder that she said the enemy army was cowering in fear.

RAHAB'S HOPE SAVED HER

If you've read the story, you know how it ends. For each of six days, the army made a single loop around the city of Jericho. On the seventh day, at the crack of dawn, Israel got up and marched around the city seven times. The priests blew the trumpets, the people gave a great shout, and the walls of Jericho collapsed before them. The army destroyed the city but saved Rahab with all her family.

Not only that, Rahab's life was transformed. Where she was once a lowly prostitute, now she was taken into the family of Israel. She made a respectable marriage, had children, and joined the list of people recognized in Matthew 1 as ancestors of the Messiah.

Rahab is a model of what we become through faith in Christ:

- Forgiven sinners
- Adopted members of the family of God
- Fulfilled and fruitful

Why? Because she acted in faith on what she knew of the word of God. What a contrast to Eve, who doubted God's word and disobeyed! When Rahab is praised in the New Testament as an example of what it means to have faith,[4] both times she's named alongside of Abraham, the father of faith. Rahab's faith had repercussions way beyond her own life. Her faith gave hope to the spies, to her family, and to the Israelites.

Thanks to the Bible, Rahab's faith still gives us hope today.

CLAIMING RAHAB'S LEGACY: FINDING COURAGE TO HANG ON TO GOD, EVEN BY A SLIM THREAD

On first glance, maybe you can't relate to Rahab. It's not often we find ourselves shut up behind city walls, fearing an attack! But maybe there's some other way your world seems to be crashing down on you. Maybe you're struggling to find a job. Maybe you have a sick child. Maybe you or a friend suffer from physical or sexual abuse or you have a loved one addicted to drugs. You might feel as if you're barely hanging on by a thread. Rahab's knowledge of who God is, his actions in history, and his plan for Israel gave her hope when her life was in danger. What do you know about God's character, works, and plan that can give you hope today with something you're facing?

When our fourth child was born, we learned he had a life-threatening heart defect. We were devastated. I'll never forget watching the doctor wheel our day-old baby away for heart surgery and wondering if we'd ever see him again. I was numb with fear. For nine months I had dreamed about this baby, building hopes and dreams, loving this child in advance—now what if he doesn't live? My heart sank to a place where I couldn't see any light. All I could feel was pain.

I sat outside the operating room door and opened my Bible. My eyes fell on Psalm 33:13, 15: "The LORD looks down from heaven, he sees all the sons of men; . . . he who fashions the hearts of them all, and observes all their deeds."

"He who fashions the hearts of them all"—that line jumped off the page. God, the creator of all things, the God who knit our son together in my womb and gave him life, fashioned his heart.

I know God didn't purposely create a defective heart. That sort of thing is a result of the Fall. But God allowed that in the child he gave us. He entrusted him to us, knowing what the situation would be. I thought of Psalm 139, which tells how God created each person and wrote down in his book all the days that were formed for us. "How precious to me are thy thoughts, O God!" The Psalmist continues, "How vast is the sum of them!" (Ps 139:17).

As I read, I felt as if God was throwing me a lifeline. He reminded me that he created our son and loves him even more than we do. That he created him with a purpose—and even planned the number of his days. And when he created him, he gave him to us to take care of, for however long he is with us, whether that is an hour, a few days, or a lifetime. Our job is to love him and be the best parents we can be while he is with us.

That quiet reminder of who God is and of his loving care strengthened my faith and opened a window of hope in my heart. Our son got through that crisis. But even if he hadn't, whatever the outcome, I was assured in that moment that God loves that boy and has a plan that will end in goodness. Even if we don't understand it, this side of heaven, we can trust and hope in him.

Many years after Rahab lived, Israel turned away from God, and when they wouldn't turn back, God allowed the Babylonians to invade and take the people into exile. Shortly before he did, he sent a message through the prophet Jeremiah: "For I know the plans I have for you," he said, "plans for welfare and not for evil, to give you a future and a hope" (Jer 29:11). Things didn't look good—they were about to lose everything, including their homeland—and yet God gave them hope to carry them through their exile. Those who knew him—and remembered his deeds—could trust in the future restoration he promised.

Who is your God? In whom or in what do you put your trust? Our God, unlike the false gods of Canaan, isn't limited to sending water, controlling floods, or prospering bank accounts. He isn't a god of our making or a deity to bribe with gifts. He's not a cosmic watchmaker who then left us alone. He's not an energy field behind the universe. He is "God in heaven above and on earth beneath" (Jos 2:11), as Rahab attested. He's the God who puts up with our faults and shows mercy again and again. He's the God who died for us and who works tirelessly to bless us.

Peter Kreeft writes that faith in God and the hope that it brings "is not a wish or a feeling, it's a rock-solid certainty, a guarantee, an anchor."[5] Our faith is solid because our God is solid. He is faithful, sure, forever. If we want to have faith, we must get to know God and his character. We have the strong witness of Rahab and many others to God's faithful love—to his provision, protection, wisdom, strength, and compassion. Read the Bible. Read the lives of the saints. Remember the things God has done for you. Plunge your roots into the nourishing soil of the sacraments. Go to adoration and Confession. Pray. Spend time with God and get to know him. God is the same today as he always was. He is here for us now as he was there for Rahab.

"Faith is the assurance of things hoped for," Hebrews 11:1 says. Faith gives us the basis we need, the substance we need, to hope in God, however dark it gets. When we take our faith and direct it toward the future like Rahab's scarlet cord, it gives us hope for ourselves and hope we can share with others. Just like my grandmother's faith, which she showed when she threw open those windows and shouted that God was in control, gave hope to her family.

St. Peter writes, "Always be prepared to make a defense to anyone who calls you to account for the hope that is in you" (1 Pt 3:15). We live in a world without hope, outside of God. The Good News of the Gospel is that yes, there *is* hope! If we have faith in Jesus, we should be some of the most hope-filled people around. The more we know him and what he's done for us, and the more we trust in him and his promises, the more we will hold steady even if the world around us falls apart. We can be beacons of hope to those around us, extending a rope to those who are lost.

QUESTIONS FOR REFLECTION

- What in Helen's or Rahab's story resonates with you?
- When have you had to cling to God to help you get through a kind of storm in your life? How did he help you?
- In what particular way is God calling you to trust him today?
- What did you learn from Rahab that might strengthen your hope?

DEBORAH

GOD CALLS US TO THE LEADERSHIP OF LOVE

> Now Deborah, a prophetess, . . . used to sit under the palm of Deborah between Ramah and Bethel in the hill country of Ephraim; and the people of Israel came up to her for judgment.
>
> —Judges 4:4–5

> In the days of Jael, caravans ceased
>   and travelers kept to the byways.
> The peasantry ceased in Israel, they ceased
>   until you arose, Deborah,
>   arose as a mother in Israel.
>
> —Judges 5:6–7

My family hasn't always been as strong in faith as it might seem from the stories I've told. In fact, Mother would be the first to tell you that living by faith isn't a one-and-done deal; it's a daily walk through light and dark, and sometimes we veer off course. For several years while I was in middle school, my parents abandoned their faith altogether. At ten years old, I didn't mind: No more church! Fewer rules! I wasn't old enough to see the hurt and alienation they caused for other family members. I wasn't old enough to know the trouble we were in as a result of their decisions. But the fact is, we *were* in trouble, the odds were against us, and nobody knew what to do.

Thank God for grandmothers.

Specifically, thank God for my great-grandma Jennie, who wasn't about to see her girl go down without a fight.

My mother's grandma Jennie lived thousands of miles away from us in California. But finding herself within a day's drive from the farm where we were moving, and not far from my dad's parents, she went to their house and knocked on the door. "John and Grace," she announced to my astonished grandparents, "can you take me to Joe and Arlita's new place? We have a battle to fight!" Armed with the fear of God and a thousand tiny strips of paper, each bearing the single word *Hallelujah*, she meant to take that property by storm.

I can just picture her, Grandma Jennie with her snowy hair in a braid piled high on her head, wearing one of her long dresses and a flower pinned on her breast, her black purse stuffed with Hallelujahs. I imagine her taking both of my grandparents by the arm and walking the perimeter of that forty-acre farm, tucking those slips of paper into every nook and cranny of the property as they went. Talk about a prayer warrior! It was her way of claiming territory for God—not too different from the way we Catholics sprinkle holy water in a place, or blessed salt. I can see them stop at every tree and fence post, then every window ledge and flower pot, saying a prayer, shouting "Hallelujah!" and then tucking a slip of paper in a crack.

A week later when we pulled into the driveway, my brothers and I tumbled out of the car to explore our new home. Not ten feet away, we found the first Hallelujah on the mailbox. Another poked out from under the welcome mat. And there, right on the doorknob, a sticker written in French: *Dieu n'est pas loin.* "God is not far off."

For months we found those tiny messages of hope. For that's what they were. Nobody else knew what to make of them, but Mom knew. Her grandma had been there. Those Hallelujahs were her signature. The sticker in French meant Dad's parents had been there too. They had not rejected us; they were praying. Their faith gave Mom faith. It reminded her that God—who loves even those who leave him—wasn't far off, with the strength that they needed to return.

GETTING THE CONTEXT

Before he died, Joshua made the people choose whether they'd keep following Yahweh or serve the gods of the neighboring people. "The Lord our God we will serve"! they swore. But the people forgot about God. They forgot to tell their kids the things that God had done for them. And as that generation passed away, so did their knowledge of God (see Judges 2:10).

For the next several centuries, Israel struggled to maintain control of the Promised Land. As they forgot God, so too they forgot the rules he'd given them to live by. They stopped trusting that God had their best interests at heart, as Adam and Eve did before them. A refrain that echoes through the final chapters of the book of Judges sums up the time period: "In those days there was no king in Israel; every man did what was right in his own eyes" (17:6, 21:25; see also 18:1, 19:1).

As a result, Israel cycled through a pattern of infidelity and rebellion that put them into the power of their neighbors. When they'd had enough, they cried for help, and God in his mercy raised up a "judge" to deliver them. The judge restored peace that lasted as long as they continued to serve God. When they stopped, the cycle began again.

This happened a dozen times that we know of. Each time, the Lord chose an unlikely person to save his people. Shamgar, for example, was a farmer (Jgs 3:31). Gideon was a coward from an insignificant family (Jgs 6:15–16). Jephthah was the son of a harlot (Jgs 11:1). And Samson, well, we all know about Samson and Delilah.

One of the least likely of the judges, because she was a woman, was also the brightest star in this motley crew. She's the only one of the twelve who was what we today would call a judge, as in someone who settles disputes. The others were more like military leaders. Deborah stands out for her wisdom, openness, and obedience to God. Like Rahab, she acted on what she believed. She heard and declared the word of God. She stands with Moses and Samuel as one of three people in the Old Testament who were not only judges but also prophets. Unlike her contemporaries, she did what was right in *God's* eyes and called others to do the same.

Jael, another woman, took part in the victory that Deborah initiated. Remember what God said to the serpent when he cursed him after the Fall? "I will put enmity between you and the woman, and between your seed and her seed; he shall bruise your head, and you shall bruise his heel" (Gn 3:15). "The woman" is an integral part of the battle against evil and is instrumental in the victory. Ever since Eve, "mother of all living," we've been watching for the "seed of the woman." Now comes Deborah, "a mother in Israel" who wages war against the enemy of God's children—and Jael, who crushes the enemy's head.

Here's the story.

DEBORAH'S STORY

You can read about Deborah in Judges 4 and 5.

For twenty years, the Canaanites had been persecuting the Israelites. A whole generation didn't know freedom or peace. The opposing general, Sisera, had command of nine hundred iron chariots and plenty of soldiers to man them.[1] Under his orders, the army patrolled the highways and plains. The people kept to the side roads and fled to the hills where chariots couldn't follow.

About ten miles north of Jerusalem, up in the hill country, "Deborah, a prophetess, the wife of Lappidoth" (Jgs 4:4) held court under a palm tree. People brought her their disputes and complaints. She gave advice and administered justice. I expect she got an earful about the cruelty of the Canaanites. The Israelites had had it with Sisera and his chariots, and were crying to God for help. Maybe they were coming to realize that doing what was right in their own eyes didn't get them very far.

DEBORAH RISES AS A "MOTHER IN ISRAEL"

Deborah felt the people's pain and saw the lack of leadership they struggled under. She also knew that God had commanded a man named Barak to gather ten thousand men to fight Sisera in the plains of Megiddo. The odds were against them. Israel had few weapons (Jgs 5:8), and none fit to send against a single chariot, not to mention nine hundred chariots with spikes spinning from their wheels. God's battle plan involved mustering poorly armed men on top of Mount Tabor and then sending them down to the plains by the Kishon River where the enemy would have the field advantage. It's hard to blame Barak for doing nothing. But Deborah trusted God to fight on their behalf, whatever the odds.

Deborah summoned Barak and repeated God's word to him: "The LORD, the God of Israel, commands you, 'Go'"! (Jgs 4:6). She said God would draw Sisera out to meet them by the river and he would give the enemy troops into their hands.

Barak agreed, but barely. "If you're so confident," he told her, "put your money where your mouth is. I'll go if you go. And only then" (see Judges 4:8).

I suppose Deborah could have despised Barak for his weakness. She could have threatened him or told him to man up and get out there himself. But like a mother who helps her child do something hard the first time, Deborah agreed to go with him. That she trusted God enough to go gave Barak the courage to lead the troops into battle. They would be victorious—but he wouldn't get the glory. As Deborah told him, the Lord would defeat Sisera by the hand of a woman. "Then Deborah arose . . ." (Jgs 4:9). She was a woman of action, not just of words. She went with Barak, and together they summoned Israel to battle.

DEBORAH RALLIES THE TROOPS

The response was an enormous accomplishment and a testimony to the respect the people had for Deborah. In her victory song after the fact, she would thank the Lord for the way the people willingly volunteered their lives. Her heart went out to them, she sang (Jgs 5:2, 9). Deborah was a strong leader with the heart of a mother. (Or maybe her mother's heart made her a strong leader!) She asked the people to volunteer for what must have seemed a hopeless cause. But ten thousand men came from six of the twelve tribes. It was the broadest coalition gathered by any judge during that time period. Why would they go, if not convinced by her word that God wasn't far off and would fight for them?

Deborah and Barak led the troops to the top of Mount Tabor, which commands a clear view of the Jezreel Valley. When Sisera gathered his chariots by the river below them, it must have been terrifying. Yet Deborah spurred Barak on. "Up!" she said. "For this is the day in which the LORD has given Sisera into your hand. Does not the LORD go out before you?" (Jgs 4:14). Barak led the troops, but it was Deborah who picked the time, gave the order to start, and fortified Barak with the assurance that God would go before them.

Strengthened by Deborah's faith, Barak led ten thousand men down the side of the hill, heedless of the iron chariots prepared to pick them off as they reached the plain. And God went before them. It was as if the stars themselves fought against Sisera (Jgs 5:20), as Deborah sang later in her song. Just as the Red Sea swallowed Pharaoh's chariots all those years before, the Kishon River flooded its banks, bogging down the chariots and leaving the Canaanite soldiers defenseless against the advancing wave of Israelites.

I love this picture of faith. First Deborah's faith, as she believed God's word and fearlessly declared it to Barak, then accompanied him and encouraged him to obey. (I wonder how history might have been different if Adam had stuck to what he'd heard and encouraged Eve.) Then Barak's faith. He accepted the word that came from the prophetess, assented, and went forward in trust. Finally, we see the faith of the people in their leaders, which enabled them to risk their lives.

DEBORAH'S PROPHECY FULFILLED BY A WOMAN

While Barak and company dealt with the soldiers and chariots, Sisera fled on foot. He took refuge in the tent of Jael, the wife of a Kenite man who had made peace with the Canaanites. Jael lured the general into her tent, gave him milk, and covered him with a rug. He told her to deny he was there if anyone asked, and then he fell asleep from exhaustion. But Jael drove a tent peg into his temple while he lay sleeping, killing him on the spot. She then turned his body over to Barak, humiliating the enemy and fulfilling Deborah's prophecy.

Origen of Alexandria saw Jael's defeat of Sisera as a picture of the Church that conquers the enemy with "the sharp point and power of the wood of the cross."[2] And when Deborah went on to immortalize Jael's deed by singing "Most blessed of women be Jael," her words would be echoed centuries later in Elizabeth's cry on greeting the pregnant Mary: "Blessed are you among women!" (Lk 1:42). Mary being, of course, the woman to whom all these others merely point,[3] the woman whose seed, with his Cross, definitively crushes the serpent's head.

But getting back to Deborah . . .

DEBORAH'S SONG SHOWS HER FEMININE GIFTS

When everything was over, Deborah and Barak led the people in a song of victory that is recorded in Judges 5:2, 6–7:

> That the leaders took the lead in Israel,
>   that the people offered themselves willingly,

> bless the LORD! . . .
> in the days of Jael, caravans ceased
> and travelers kept to the byways.
> The peasantry ceased in Israel, they ceased
> until you arose, Deborah,
> arose as a mother in Israel.

Those are just a few lines of the song, which is one of the oldest biblical texts that we have. Scholars think it was written soon after the victory, in the second millennium BC. It's classic Hebrew poetry and the best-known biblical victory song.

A few things to note about it:

- Deborah and Barak both sing, but it's commonly known as the "Song of Deborah" due to her prominent role in the victory.
- The words of the song reveal the feminine gifts Deborah brought to bear on what is often considered a masculine task.

For example, the song starts not with the glory of the fight and the victory but by praising those who offered their lives. Deborah was sensitive to how hard it must have been for the leaders under Barak to lead, and for the people to follow, given the odds against them. After going on to explain how dire the situation was, with people weaponless and hiding in the hills, she sang, "My heart goes out to [those] who offered themselves willingly" (Jgs 5:9). She then applauded the sacrifice of the six tribes who sent help, contrasting it to those tribes that didn't (Jgs 5:15–16). The people were individuals to her, not cogs in a military machine.

This is the feminine genius at work, the ʻezer we read about in Genesis 2:20, where Eve was created to be a "helper fit for" Adam, which we saw could mean sustaining him in times of danger, or delivering, protecting, and upholding life. It turns out that classically feminine strengths such as sensitivity and putting people first are valuable in war as well as peace.

- Most curious, Deborah is memorialized in the song not as a judge or a prophetess but as something very different. Life as they knew it practically stopped, the song says, "until Deborah arose as *a mother in Israel*" (Jgs 5:7, emphasis mine).

There's nothing in the Bible to indicate that Deborah was a "mother" in the sense of bearing children. She's called "the wife of Lappidoth" (Jgs 4:4), but the Hebrew, *eshet Lapidot*, can equally be translated "woman of torches." Figuratively speaking, she's like a torch that lit a fire under Barak (which means "lightning"). Whether she is married or has biological children or not has nothing to do with her role in this battle. That she is a "mother in Israel" must mean something else. What might that be?

Deborah means "bee" in Hebrew, and maybe there's something here of the queen bee raising the swarm to protect the hive. We already saw how she cared for the welfare of the people. Deborah's greatness wasn't in fighting and conquering but in the motherly qualities of protecting and teaching, advising and encouraging, spurring on to the obedience of faith.

The phrase "mother in Israel" appears elsewhere in scripture. In 2 Samuel 20, it's applied to a city that has been besieged by King David's commander Joab. A wise woman calls out and reminds him that people have been coming for years to that city for counsel and to have disputes settled, like quarreling children go to their mother to decide their argument. "You seek to destroy a city which is *a mother in Israel*," she says. "Why will you swallow up the heritage of the LORD?" (2 Sm 20:19, emphasis mine). Her action saved the city. Like both the woman and the city, Deborah was a wise judge known for her counsel, who spoke the word of the Lord to the powerful and saved them.

CLAIMING DEBORAH'S LEGACY: "DO AS HE TELLS YOU"

The quality that identifies us physically as women—that we are biologically capable of bearing and nursing children—points to an innate spiritual identification as well. Women have a special "genius," as Pope John Paul II called it, of attending to other people and seeing their goodness, of being sensitive to their needs and moving to help them, of lifting the fallen, of nurturing life. "Motherhood concerns the whole person," he writes, "not just the body" (*Mulieris Dignitatem*, 4). It plunges women—whether or not they are biological mothers—into the center of God's plan to love and rescue humanity and helps give that plan hands and feet in the world.[4]

Jesus drew attention to another aspect of motherhood in his answer to the woman who called out from the crowd to say, "Blessed is the womb that bore you, and the breasts that you sucked!" (Lk 11:27). Without denigrating biological motherhood, he pointed out the deeper meaning it reveals: "Blessed rather are those who hear the word of God and keep it!" (Lk 11:28).

Both, of course, describe his mother. Mary bore the Son of God, but she did so because first she *heard* and *kept* the Word of God in her heart, allowing it to bear fruit within her. Pope John Paul II points out that this gospel helps us understand that "*the motherhood* of every woman . . . is similarly not only 'of flesh and blood': it expresses a profound '*listening to the word of the living God*' and a readiness to 'safeguard' this Word" (*Mulieris Dignitatem*, 19, emphasis in original).

All of which brings me back to Deborah, "a mother in Israel." What a great title! She is "mother" not only for the reasons I named above but also because she heard and kept the word of God. She also helped Barak to keep it, in spite of his fear and reluctance to act.

I can remember my mother saying to us, when we ignored something she said, "Listen to me!" To which we often replied, "I heard you." That wasn't the answer she was looking for. If we didn't say something like "Yes, Mother," and get doing what she had asked, the next thing we'd hear was often a warning. "Delayed obedience is disobedience" was her favorite. It was her way of saying, ". . . or else!"

Mothers teach us obedience. Ideally they teach us obedience to the Word of God. Think again of Mary, this time at the wedding at Cana (see John 2). Her mother's heart notices the lack of wine and what it will mean to the hosts and the guests, and she goes to her Son for help. Even before he turns jars of water to wine, she turns to the servants and says, "Do whatever he tells you" (Jn 2:5).

Isn't that what we see Deborah doing in Israel? She noticed the plight of the people and her heart went out to them. From her seat under the palm tree, where they came to her for judgment and where I assume she sought the Lord's wisdom, she heard the word of the Lord. Immediately, she summoned Barak and told him to do what the Lord had told him. Then like a wise mother who helps a child do something difficult by standing by him but not doing the work—she went with Barak into battle, encouraged him, spurred him on to trust God and do what looked impossible. Because of her he reached his own greatness. Barak moved from doing what was right in his own eyes to a radical following of God's surprising, even counterintuitive directions. Her faith gave him faith.

Fr. Gerald Vann, O.P., in his lovely book *Eve and the Gryphon*, writes about the vocation of motherhood and what he calls "the leadership of love," that it "not only teaches; it spurs to action; it leads."[5] He writes, "It is the destiny of woman to form man, by her active leadership, into the likeness of Christ, to help him to return to the source of life, and knowledge, and power: . . . It is her destiny to show man, by being herself God's handmaid, how to rise to the fulness of his stature. . . . How is she to do all this? By the twofold office of love: by teaching; and by empowering, encouraging, drawing onwards to life."[6]

This describes my grandma Jennie, I think, who did what it took to remind my parents of the nearness of God and his power. Her action gave them the courage they needed to fight for the life of our family. It aptly describes Deborah as well, and I hope one day it will describe you and me. That we will have ears open to God's Word and *hear*, not just listen. That we will allow it to take root in our hearts and bear the fruit that God desires and also proclaim that Word to others. That we will walk beside those who are reluctant or afraid and remind them that God is nearby, encouraging them to "do as he tells you." That we will do our part to achieve spiritually the kind of victory over the devil that Jael's tent peg so graphically portrays.

The world needs mothers like Deborah as much as it needs male leaders. To quote Fr. Vann again (and I highly recommend his little book): "The safety and salvation of the world depend on the combined work of man and woman alike; if either fails the world must fail; but it remains true that we in this age have been living under a system in which the masculine mind predominates, and we desperately need the fullness of the vocation of woman. She shall crush the head of the serpent."[7]

QUESTIONS FOR REFLECTION

- What about Jennie's or Deborah's story resonates with you? How have you experienced something similar?
- While not all of us are called to be prophets, each of us experiences a time of war (whether external or internal) when we must stand strong. When have you shown such strength in your own life?
- In what particular way is God calling you to be a "mother in Israel" today?
- How are you encouraged to make better use of your feminine gifts?

RUTH

GOD'S KINGDOM HAS ROOM FOR US ALL

> But Ruth said, "Entreat me not to leave you
> or to return from following you; for where you
> go I will go, and where you lodge I will lodge;
> your people shall be my people, and your
> God my God."
>
> —Ruth 1:16

As I turned twenty-one, I was all set to go to Oxford. Home of J. R. R. Tolkien, C. S. Lewis, and T. S. Eliot; backdrop to *Brideshead Revisited* and *Howards End*—all my dreams, as I graduated college with a major in English lit, were wrapped up in that magical place. And I was going there to study! It was such an answer to prayer, everything from the timing to my acceptance to raising the money to go. At last the tuition had been paid and my plane ticket purchased; all that remained was to finish some pre-class reading and pack my bags.

Then the news came. My grandma Helen had cancer. In those days, overseas travel wasn't something you did lightly, at least not on my budget. I planned to stay a long time. If I went to England, who knew if I would see Grandma again?

I was in agony. What should I do? Follow my dreams or my heart? Common sense said to follow my dreams. Grandma was excited for me; she wouldn't want me to change just for her. And if I pulled out, I'd lose the money and my spot in the program, and let down everyone who helped me. Worst of all, the chance might never come again. *God,* I prayed, *what is the right thing to do?*

It was my aunt Andrea who saw my misery and sat down with me to help me sort it out. In the end, I did the hard thing. I canceled my trip to England and moved to Denver to help care for Grandma. "And that has made all the difference," to quote Robert Frost.[1]

I never did get to study at Oxford, never had the adventure I'd imagined, never did the things I'd hoped to do back then. Instead, I spent that critical post-college, coming-of-age time with my grandparents. For two years I saw up close and personal what happens when a woman of faith stares death in the face. Her body began to fail. It cracked like a clay pot under the strain. And—surprise, surprise!—light poured out of the cracks.

I'll never forget rushing in to check on her late one night when I heard her loud sobs—only to find she was crying in prayer for people she knew, who needed help. That light I saw was the light of Christ. Grandma had spent so many years in prayer and filling herself with the Word of God that it truly transformed her.

I don't know if anyone will ever see something like that in me. I can only hope. But I know that if they do, I will have caught that light from her. Because I got close enough to catch the spark, her God is my God too.

Thinking of that decision I made to set aside my own hopes and plans out of love for my grandmother, and realizing how God in his providence has made up in unexpected ways for what I left behind, I think of Ruth in the Old Testament. Ruth was an ordinary girl who was rewarded for loving and caring for someone instead of putting her own interests first. Ruth found God through simple steps of kindness. She is proof of Jesus' words in Matthew 6:33 that if we seek first his kingdom and his righteousness, God will provide.

GETTING THE CONTEXT

Ruth is one of just three books of the Bible that are named for women. The other two, Esther and Judith, we will look at in future chapters. Ruth is also the only book of the Bible named for a Gentile, male or female. The Jewish tradition showcases its four short chapters by reading them every year at Shavuot (the Feast of Weeks).[2]

What is so important about Ruth that she should be honored this way? The purpose of Shavuot gives us a clue. Along with Passover and the Feast of Tabernacles, it's one of three annual pilgrim feasts at which attendance was required. It celebrated God's provision in the harvest, and people were to show their gratefulness by allowing the poor to glean from the edges of their fields (see Leviticus 23:22–23). The book of Ruth shows this practice, but it wasn't chosen just for that reason. Over time, Shavuot came to celebrate the giving of the Torah to Israel at Mount Sinai after the exodus. That was the time when God took Israel as his people and they took him as their God. The Ten Commandments were part of a covenant—wedding vows, if you will—that defined their relationship. Because of this, the Jews consider Shavuot to be the anniversary of their marriage to God.

It's all well and good for the Jews as a people to pledge themselves to God, but that commitment must be renewed on an individual basis by each person who is born. Ruth is the quintessential convert. Like Rahab, she is a shining example of someone who as a foreigner, separated from the family of God, nevertheless sought him out and cleaved to him. As a result, Ruth was richly rewarded—married by a man who redeemed her and made her a bona fide member of the family of God. Ultimately her yes to God gave rise to a new line from which came King David and the Messiah, Jesus Christ, who would redeem the world.

Like Deborah's story, the book of Ruth is set in the tumultuous time of the judges. In it, a family from Bethlehem is forced by famine to leave Israel. They emigrate to Moab, the area that today is called Jordan. It's there that they meet Ruth, who later follows them home; and this unlikely foreigner injects hope into the story of God's people.

RUTH'S STORY

You can read about Ruth in the book of Ruth.

I don't know what Ruth, a Moabite, saw in Mahlon, the foreigner from across the Dead Sea who came to her country with his parents and brother seeking food. There had been hostility between Moab and Israel since the days of Moses, and no Moabite was allowed to enter the assembly of Israel. I assume the rivalry went both ways. Why the parents of Ruth and Orpah gave them in marriage to enemy refugees is anyone's guess.

But marry them off they did. Ruth and Orpah joined Mahlon and Chilion and their recently widowed mother, Naomi. Ten years later, both men died childless, leaving the women extremely vulnerable. Without husbands or sons to care for them, they were doomed to poverty, even possible starvation.

One day Naomi received word that there was food again in Bethlehem. She set out for home, taking the young women with her. But then she had second thoughts. In those days, when a man died leaving a childless widow behind, his brother or close relative would marry her. This was necessary if the woman was to be provided for as well as to preserve the husband's line and property. But Naomi was beyond child-bearing age, too old for a husband (Ru 1:12).

Naomi looked at Ruth and Orpah and knew they'd be better off staying home. However much she had come to rely on them, however much she loved them, she must send them away. "Go back," she said. "Go home and find new husbands. You've been kind to me and mine—now may the Lord be kind to you and give you a home" (see Ruth 1:8–9).

RUTH CHOOSES NAOMI AND NAOMI'S GOD

Earlier we saw the deep emptiness that can come with not having children or the love of a husband. Leah suffered from not being loved; Rachel was tormented by not having children. Those are very painful things, to be sure. But Ruth and Orpah had *nothing*. They had lost good husbands, and neither had children; they had no prospects whatsoever. Imagine the anguish! Think back to a time when you suffered loss. What was in your mind? Was there anything beyond sadness and self-preservation?

Orpah did the sensible thing. After a tearful farewell and a kiss goodbye, she returned to her people and the hope of another life. But Ruth clung to Naomi. "Go on. Go back with Orpah," the older woman said (see Ruth 1:15). Whereupon Ruth poured out her loving determination to stick by Naomi, no matter what. She begged Naomi not to ask her to leave: "Entreat me not to leave you or to return from following you; for where you go I will go, and where you lodge I will lodge; your people shall be my people, and your God my God; where you die I will die, and there will I be buried. May the LORD do so to me and more also if even death parts me from you" (Ru 1:16–17).

Isn't it interesting that these words that have been proclaimed at thousands of weddings were first said to a mother-in-law! For better or worse, Ruth set aside her own personal interests and threw her lot in with Naomi.

I can't imagine why Ruth would do this, except out of love. Love of Naomi, which grew into love for Naomi's God. This astounds me. Naomi complained of emptiness and the bitter hand God had dealt her. A decade before, she and her husband, Elimelech, fled a land that was suffering divine punishment for sin. From then on, Naomi knew nothing but a continued stripping away of blessing. I can only think that in the middle of all of that, she still found it in her heart to praise the Lord. Like the prophet Habakkuk centuries later, who, facing the Babylonian invasion, said that even if all produce fails and food is gone, "yet I will rejoice in the LORD, I will joy in the God of my salvation" (Hb 3:18).

How else, except by their example, would Ruth come to this determined desire to take on Naomi's God, to take refuge under his wings (Ru 2:12)? Their faithful example bore the sweet fruit of love and compassion. It seems to me that however great Ruth's need and sorrow might have been, she saw that her mother-in-law's need was even greater. Naomi had lost her country, her husband, and two sons, and she was too old for a new start. She was feeling bitter that she couldn't help her daughters-in-law. She felt that the Lord had brought her misfortune. Seeing her despair, Ruth clung to her and said she'd stay with her for life. By setting aside her own needs and reaching out in love, she saved herself.

Ruth exemplifies the kind of love St. Paul described when he urged Christians to "do nothing from selfishness or conceit, but in humility count others better than yourselves. Let each of you look not only to his own interests, but also to the interests of others. Have this mind among yourselves, which was in Christ Jesus" (Phil 2:3–5).

Ruth left behind her own family, land, and gods in exchange for a future that in all likelihood would mean childless widowhood in an unknown land where she might not be welcome. She also took on Naomi's God, whom she trusted despite Naomi's negative experiences.

Naomi painted a black picture of the future, saying there was no hope for Ruth where she was going. In a courageous display of faith, Ruth linked arms with her mother-in-law and headed into the dark.

GOD AT WORK BEHIND THE SCENES

I've spoken already of my grandma Helen, whose faith kept shining through the dark of terminal cancer. Many years previously, she and Grandpa fled Communist Shanghai with six small children and little more than the clothes on their backs. Grandma had a saying that's become a kind of family motto for us: "Don't be afraid to paint the picture as black as it really is," she'd say when things got bad. "Just don't forget to write across that picture, '*but God*'"—as in, "I am about to die, *but God* will be with you" (Gn 48:21, emphasis mine); or, "the author of life you put to death, *but God* raised him from the dead" (Acts 3:15, NABRE; emphasis mine).

The Bible is full of examples like that: times when everything looked hopeless, but God came through with his mercy and providential love. Ruth's story is one of them. My own life is full of *but God* moments—times when God worked through stress in our marriage to draw Mark and me closer together, for example. Or the time we made it through losing a job and our house only to find God had been with us all along, saving us from a bad situation we didn't see and pointing us toward better things.

The book of Ruth is a place I can go to when new fear makes me forget times God has been there for me and my family in the past. You can see him at work behind the scenes in Ruth and Naomi's situation, even if Naomi can't. It was God who made the land of Israel productive again, and providential that the women arrived in Bethlehem at the start of the barley harvest (Ru 1:22). It was God who preserved Boaz, an unmarried "kinsman of her husband's, a man of wealth" (Ru 2:1), and prepared him to be the answer to their need.[3] And it was thanks to divine providence that as Ruth set off into the fields to glean behind the reapers, "she happened to come to the part of the field belonging to Boaz" (Ru 2:3) just as he arrived there from Bethlehem.

But I'm getting ahead of myself.

RUTH'S LOVING CARE FOR NAOMI

Naomi's reappearance in Bethlehem after a decade of absence created an uproar. "The whole town was stirred because of them" (Ru 1:19). I expect Ruth could hear the women talking: *Is this really Naomi, who left because of the famine? But where's Elimelech? And those two nice boys of theirs? What happened?* Then she watched as Naomi settled in with those people who knew her name by asking them to change it. Naomi means "pleasant," but she asked them to call her Mara ("bitter") instead; for "the Almighty has brought calamity upon me" (Ru 1:20–21).

Ruth did all she could to help her mother-in-law, starting with looking for food. Soon she was making an impression on the town. As the new girl, I expect all eyes were on her. Everyone had an opinion, and not just the women. The man in charge of the reapers noticed that she arrived early in the morning to work and didn't rest. He remarked on her polite humility and praised her diligence (Ru 2:6–7).

Boaz, the landowner, offered Ruth a safe place with the girls gleaning in the field. When she asked why he would take notice of her, a foreigner, he answered, "All that you have done for your mother-in-law since the death of your husband has been fully told me, and how you left your father and mother and your native land and came to a people that you did not know before" (Ru 2:11). The town's rumor mill was at work in her favor! And her actions reinforced the impression. Read Ruth's four short chapters and see that she was hardworking, loving, humble, kind, loyal, faithful, obedient, selfless, bold, patient. Ruth was an ordinary woman of extraordinary character, and everybody saw it.

Boaz continued: "The LORD recompense you for what you have done, and a full reward be given you by the LORD, the God of Israel, under whose wings you have come to take refuge!" (Ru 2:12). That was the real source of the blessing and reward Ruth received. Yes, she was good and kind to Naomi. But along with that, she sought out the God of Israel and left everything behind to take refuge in him.

As the author of Hebrews says in that great chapter on faith: "Whoever would draw near to God must believe he exists and that he rewards those who seek him" (Heb 11:6). Ruth set out toward God, not unlike the way Abraham and Sarah set out into the unknown so many years before, to follow him. That is why Boaz prayed that her faith would be rewarded. In addition, he did his part to make her work light, safe, and profitable.

RUTH REAPS LOVE'S HARVEST

When Naomi heard how Boaz had helped Ruth, and when she realized that he was a close relative, she saw a way to make Ruth secure and to continue the family line. Her plan was odd, to say the least. All the barley had been harvested, and it was time to winnow it—to toss it into the air and allow the wind to blow away the chaff. This was a job done by the men on a platform called the threshing floor, usually in the evening breeze. Naomi told Ruth to put on her finest clothes and hide near the threshing floor until the men finished eating and drinking and they lay down for the night. Go to Boaz, uncover his feet, and lie down, she said, "and he will tell you what to do" (Ru 3:4).

I have no idea what Naomi thought would happen. It sounds suggestive to me, not to mention dangerous. Maybe she counted on the way Boaz had already shown himself concerned for Ruth's welfare, to assume he wouldn't take advantage of her. Whatever she thought, Ruth took it into her own hands by speaking first. When Boaz woke up, startled, to find her at his feet, she appealed to him as "next of kin" to "spread your skirt over your maidservant" (Ru 3:9). But she wasn't asking to get under his covers, as much as it sounds like that. The word she used for skirt is *kanaph*, the Hebrew word for "wing"—as in the wings of God that Boaz praised Ruth for taking refuge beneath (Ru 2:12). Elsewhere in the Bible, this figure of speech is used for taking a woman as a wife (see Ezekiel 16:8). It's clear from what Boaz says next that he understood perfectly: this was a request for marriage by the widow of his relative, to someone who could redeem that man's posterity.

I love Boaz's reply. It's like Adam's delighted response when he first saw Eve. Boaz cried, "May you be blessed by the LORD, my daughter" (Ru 3:10). He went on to explain: "Your kindness to me is even greater than the kindness you showed Naomi, because you easily could have gone after one of the young men. And you chose me!" He was so grateful, you can feel it. "Now don't be afraid," he continued. "I'll do everything you're asking" (see Ruth 3:10–11). Why? "For all my fellow townsmen know that you are a woman of worth" (Ru 3:11). Ruth was a treasure, and Boaz knew it.

Boaz was a treasure too. How many men would spend the night with a woman he loved and not touch her? That's exactly what Boaz did. He knew there was someone closer in line with the first right of refusal. He let her sleep, then sent her off before anyone could see she'd been there. Then he went to the town gates where business was done; he found that nearer relative, made sure he didn't want to redeem what had been lost to Elimilech's line, then bought the family's land himself and claimed Ruth as his wife in front of the elders.

The witnesses at the gate pronounced a blessing: "May the LORD make [Ruth] . . . like Rachel and Leah, who together built up the house of Israel. May you [Boaz] prosper . . . because of the children that the LORD will give you by this young woman" (Ru 4:11–12).

Soon Ruth and Boaz had a son named Obed, from whom would come Jesse, father of King David, forerunner of the Messiah. Matthew records this in his genealogy of Jesus, and adds an interesting fact: Boaz's mother (or other female ancestor) was Rahab, the Canaanite prostitute who gave shelter to the spies. Perhaps Boaz's kindness to Ruth came from faith passed down from Rahab, another outsider brought into God's family. God may have worked through her legacy, preparing Boaz and holding him in wait for this young Moabite widow who would inject her faith into a nation that was losing theirs.

CLAIMING RUTH'S LEGACY: SEEK GOD'S KINGDOM AND YOU WILL BE FILLED

You may have heard of the "Proverbs 31 woman." In the evangelical circles I grew up in, she was the model woman we all wanted to be (or were supposed to be but didn't think we could possibly live up to). Titled "Ode to a Capable Wife" in the RSVCE, Proverbs 31:10–31 begins, "A good wife who can find? She is far more precious than jewels." It goes on to describe all her fine qualities, summed up at the end like this:

> "Many women have done excellently,
>   but you surpass them all."
> Charm is deceitful, and beauty is vain,
>   but a woman who fears the LORD is to be praised.

> Give her of the fruit of her hands,
>> and let her works praise her in the gates.
> (Prv 31:29–31)

Because the book of Ruth immediately follows this in the Hebrew Bible, it's easy to see her as the embodiment of this woman. Not only that, *good wife* in Hebrew is *eshet chayil*, which is how Boaz described Ruth when he said everyone in town knew she was "a woman of worth" (Ru 3:11). In fact, she is the only woman in scripture who is called *eshet chayil*. For this reason, many scholars think that Ruth is the model for the woman in this final chapter of Proverbs.

Eshet means "woman" or "wife"; *chayil* normally refers to a force of some kind, whether of people, means, or other resources; it's the word used for armies, for strength, wealth, and efficiency. Remember what *helpmeet* really means? *Chayil* enables that kind of "divine assistance" we saw when God created Eve! The Jewish tradition usually translates *eshet chayil* as "woman of valor."[4]

Proverbs 31 calls this woman "more precious than jewels" or pearls. What makes a pearl precious? Not only its rarity or the time it takes to create one but also the way a pearl is made. It comes in response to a tiny piece of grit lodged inside an oyster's shell. The oyster responds by coating the irritant with layer after layer of nacre until a smooth and radiant globe is formed. In the same way, kindness can be wrapped around an insult or injustice. Forgiveness softens rough edges. Returning love for harm transforms injury into a thing of lasting beauty. Pouring love onto another's need does the same thing. Like Ruth did with Naomi.

It's a paradox of the spiritual life that when we give out of our emptiness, God fills us. One day when I was living with my grandparents, they got into a heated disagreement about something. As usual, they took it into another room to resolve. *So that I don't hear them fight*, I thought to myself. But then Grandma came out of the room with a chuckle and a twinkle in her eye. "Sarah-girl," she said, "when you run out of love . . . just make some more!" I was slightly scandalized when I thought what that might mean, in practice.

But then I watched as over and over Grandma did just that. In particular, I remember the times she was in pain from radiation or chemo. How exhausted and empty she must have felt, yet invariably her solution was to think about someone else. "Help me pack up some food to take to the shelter," she might say when her stomach was too upset to eat. "Maria has those poor little children at home with no daddy. Is there a game we can take over to them?" Little things, often, but all of them sparked with love. I see now that not only did she help other people but also the more she gave, the more she was filled. As the Lord said, "give, and it will be given to you; good measure, pressed down, shaken together, running over, will be put into your lap. For the measure you give will be the measure you get back" (Lk 6:38).

This, I think, is the legacy of Ruth. She gave in love out of her emptiness, and she tucked herself under the wings of Yahweh and was filled.

QUESTIONS FOR REFLECTION

- What in Ruth's story or the author's journey resonates with you? Have you experienced something similar?
- Turn in your Bible to Proverbs 31 and read about the "woman of valor." What are some qualities about her that you would like to put into practice?
- In what small way has God called you to seek his kingdom first today?
- What did you learn from Ruth's story that might strengthen your love?

HANNAH

GOD LISTENS TO OUR PRAYERS

Hannah answered, ". . . I have been pouring out my soul before the LORD."

—1 Samuel 1:15

Hannah also prayed and said,
   "My heart exults in the LORD;
   My strength is exalted in the LORD."

—1 Samuel 2:1

When I was still a fairly new Catholic, a friend gave me a medal with an image of St. Monica imprinted on one side and St. Augustine on the other. She thought it suited me as a Bible teacher-scholar and mother of boys. Today I wear it frequently, together with medals of St. Helena, "seeker of the true Cross," and St. Walburga, missionary and patron saint of authors. I look to their examples and ask their intercession related to the three most important things in my life: my family, both biological and spiritual; my growth in faith; and my teaching, speaking, and writing.

For a long time, though, the St. Monica–St. Augustine medal lay untouched in my jewelry box. I'd spent thirty years as a Protestant suspicious of things such as medals because of my misunderstanding of Catholic devotion to the saints. Although I'd come to accept the truth of Catholic teaching, asking saints to pray wasn't something that came naturally to me. And as much as I appreciated the gift, I couldn't bring myself to wear the medal.

Until, that is, I got to know St. Monica.

Mark and I had been praying hard for one of our children, who had gotten tangled up with some bad friends and questionable activities. It was like we were watching a train barreling forward on a broken track—unless something changed, there could only be disaster ahead. I went for advice to a wise woman I knew whose children were grown. "I always ask St. Monica to pray for my kids," she said, "and to pray for me too—that I'll stay strong and keep praying." I'd never thought to ask a saint to pray. "What else is St. Monica doing up there," my friend continued, "besides worshipping God and praying for people like us? You should ask her."

I knew that Monica had prayed for decades for her profligate son, who ended up becoming a brilliant spokesman for the faith and a Doctor of the Church. Now I started reading up on her, figuring it would be easier to approach someone I knew something about. I learned that she developed a secret passion for wine when she was a young girl, but when a family slave called her out on it, she was so ashamed that she never touched a drop again (which is why people who struggle with addictions seek her prayers as well). While she was still young, Monica was married off to a pagan man with a violent temper who was critical of her faith. She met his rage with patient kindness and by the end of his life, she won him over to Christianity.

Monica's brilliant son Augustine drove her to her knees because of his loose lifestyle and his love of Manichaeism, a dualistic heresy that sees (instead of one almighty God) conflicting worlds of good spirit and evil matter. Augustine challenged his mother to give up *her* faith to overcome the split between them, but she insisted that he was the one who was out of line. The more he strayed, the more she prayed, fasted, and cried on his behalf. When she followed him to Rome, afraid he would never convert, he eluded her and moved to Milan, where he met St. Ambrose, under whose influence he eventually entered the Church. It was an answer to decades of his mother's prayers.

Wow, I thought. *Here's a woman who understands not only the brokenhearted mom but also the wayward kid. She's had troubles of her own to battle. She's not some self-righteous fanatic; she's real.* What really impressed me was that she didn't wear her worry on her sleeve, moaning and nagging at her son. She took her tears to God and left them in his care; and she never stopped praying. I want to be like that.

Monica makes me think of Hannah in the Old Testament, whose tears and prayers caught the attention of the Lord long before there was a Monica or an Augustine. The Lord answered her request by sending her a son: the great judge and prophet Samuel. Like Monica, Hannah is known for her prayers. Like Monica, her prayers contributed to the raising of a faithful, holy son. May their examples encourage us to redouble our prayers for the children in our care and for those who have no one to pray for them.

GETTING THE CONTEXT

When did people first start to pray to God? I mean really *pray,* one-on-one? Who first figured out that you could have a conversation in your mind with Someone Out There . . . that he would hear (would want to hear, would really listen) . . . and then actually respond?

I take prayer for granted; I've been talking to God all my life. Nearly everyone I know does the same, but the older I get, the more people I meet who laugh at the idea—of a God who is there, or who cares, or who listens. Or they "commune with the divine," a kind of emptying of thought to be absorbed into the Other. I'm starting to feel as if I'm in the minority, which takes me back where I started. When did people start to pray to God?

It had to be that he reached out first so we could know him, which is really what the Bible's all about. You can watch the relationship unfold as you read. Adam and Eve walked with God in the Garden; you get the feeling they chatted about their days after dinner, they were so close. All of that fell by the wayside, of course, but soon you get these beautiful glimpses of conversation as God reached out to different ones: Abraham stood before the Lord and argued him down from destroying Sodom if he could find in it ten righteous men (see Genesis 18). Jacob wrestled with God to learn who he is and be blessed (see Genesis 32). Moses spoke to God face-to-face (see Numbers 12:8)—but the very fact that the point is made shows how rare that was.

Fast-forward to the Promised Land, to the time of the judges. It was a time when people didn't teach their children about God and consequently generations grew up not knowing him. But some people did, such as Deborah, who was in tune enough to pass God's word to Barak; or Naomi, who passed her faith on to Ruth. Even in that dark time, some people still sought God and made a personal connection. Hannah is the first person in the Old Testament who shows us we can throw ourselves on God, pour out our distress, and find comfort and help. Later David will do the same, and he will give us words in the Psalms so we'll know how to do it too. But—maybe it's the feminine genius at work in her, the woman's need for relationship—Hannah is the first whose prayer we hear, not as a leader concerned for the flock but as an ordinary person like you and me. She shows us that faith involves a deeply personal connection with God.

Earlier we read about Rachel's and Leah's longing for love and children, about that empty hole we have inside that's made for God. Like Rachel, Hannah was barren. It was the intensity of her longing, rightly focused toward God, that set her heart straight. St. Augustine writes, "God wills that our desire should be exercised in prayer, that we may be able to receive what he is prepared to give."[1] Here is one of the clearest pictures in all scripture of what that kind of prayer looks like. Hannah gives us a pattern for faith-filled prayer.

HANNAH'S STORY

You can read about Hannah in 1 Samuel 1–2.

Hannah means "grace."

I'm going to go out on a limb here and say that this particular Hannah was full of grace. How else did she not retaliate against Penninah's spite?

Both women were married to Elkanah, a Levite from the hill country of Ephraim. They lived in Ramah,[2] not far, incidentally, from where Deborah once sat under her palm tree. Hannah had no children. Penninah, who was probably taken on as a second wife for this very reason, had lots of them, both girls and boys—a fact that she continued to rub Hannah's nose in, trying to provoke her.

It was a lawless time, and many had forgotten God. But there were still those who worshipped the Lord, among them Elkanah and his family. In 1 Chronicles 6 we learn that Elkanah descended from Kohath, whose clan cared for the ark of the covenant and other sacred furnishings on Israel's journey from Egypt to Canaan. Maybe that had something to do with Elkanah's regular visits to Shiloh, where the ark was kept.

Every year the family packed up and traveled there to worship the Lord and sacrifice. The custom was to burn parts of the animal, give part to the priest, and then share in some as a family. Elkanah presided over the meal, giving a portion each to Penninah and her children, and then to Hannah. How much? The ancient Greek and Hebrew texts differ. Some Bibles say he gave Hannah one portion, although he loved her, because she had no children; others say he gave Hannah a double portion, because he loved her, although she had no children. But whether it was one portion or two, Elkanah loved Hannah such that Penninah, for all her children, looked on her as a rival. Every year it was the same. Penninah provoked Hannah until she cried and wouldn't eat the meat she was given. What was meant to be a meaningful time of family worship ended in heartache.

Here's where Hannah's grace showed, even through her pain. Just compare her to Sarah, who reacted to Hagar's scorn by mistreating her. Or to Rachel, who used the fact that Jacob loved her best to put her sister down. Hannah did neither of those things, though some might think her justified if she had. Neither did she turn on Elkanah, blaming him for her situation the way Sarah blamed Abraham, or demand children lest she die, as Rachel did of Jacob (see Genesis 30:1).

If Hannah hoped to find comfort in her husband, it wasn't forthcoming. Elkanah felt her pain but didn't understand why he wasn't enough. "Hannah, why do you weep?" Elkanah asked. "And why do you not eat? And why is your heart sad? Am I not more to you than ten sons?" (1 Sm 1:8).

What Hannah needed wasn't her husband's love (not to put too little value on that). It wasn't even for Penninah to stop pestering and reminding her, because the situation wasn't going to change. Hannah didn't have a son, couldn't have a son, and her ache was so deep she couldn't be consoled.

What do you do with that kind of ache? Maybe you've felt the same pain of longing. Or of losing someone dear to you. Where do you go with the pain?

HANNAH TAKES HER SORROW TO GOD AND FINDS COMFORT

What Hannah needed was God, and she knew it. When the meal was done, she got up and went before the Lord. "She was deeply distressed and prayed to the LORD, and wept bitterly. And she vowed a vow and said, O LORD of hosts, if thou wilt indeed look on the affliction of thy maidservant, and remember me, and not forget thy maidservant, but wilt give to thy maidservant a son, then I will give him to the LORD all the days of his life" (1 Sm 1:10–11).

Hannah was so upset, so intent on her prayer as she poured out her heart and soul to the Lord, she was hardly aware of anything around her. It was as if she was all alone with him; her eyes were closed and she spoke from her heart—her lips moved, but she didn't make a sound. The intensity of her prayer made her stand out. The old priest, Eli, was watching her. He was so used to the kind of women who visited his immoral sons there at the tabernacle, he thought she was drunk. "Sober up!" he told her, interrupting her prayer (see 1 Samuel 1:14). But he changed his tune when she told him how troubled and anxious she was. "'Go in peace, and the God of Israel grant your petition,'" he said. "Then the woman went her way and ate, and her countenance was no longer sad" (1 Sm 1:17, 18).

"Her countenance was no longer sad"—her face, instead of being red, blotchy, and tear-stained with grief, became a serene reflection of a soul at peace. No more distress, no more anguish, no more bitter longing. That was all gone. Read on, and you'll see they got up early the next day and worshiped. They went home and before long, Hannah got pregnant. God gave her a son, but even before that, he healed her heart.

HANNAH ENTRUSTS HER CHILD TO GOD

Hannah named her baby Samuel, because God heard her prayer and answered. She nursed the child lovingly until he was weaned, then fulfilled her vow. She took him to Shiloh "that he may appear in the presence of the LORD, and abide there forever" (1 Sm 1:22).

It's not easy to give children into other people's care. Yet Hannah gave up her miracle child after just a few years and left him with a man whose own sons, both priests, were "worthless men" with "no regard for the LORD," who bullied people for choice portions of meat offered in sacrifice, ignored their father, and slept with the women who served at the tent of meeting (see 1 Samuel 2:12–17, 22–25).

How did she do it? How do parents today send kids to college, knowing that many will lose their faith there? Or how do they send boys to seminary, with so many rumors of abuse? People asked us that when we sent our son. We're fortunate to have a fine seminary, with many fine priests. But the question remains, in this climate. As parents, we do our best; we entrust them to God, and we pray. Hannah helped me with that. She and Elkanah must have known what kind of men served at Shiloh. Yet when Samuel was weaned, they took him to the temple with a thank offering and presented him to Eli. They gave the boy to the Lord forever. Talk about faith!

HANNAH EXULTS IN THE LORD

What strikes me about the tone of Hannah's worship, for we have the words of her prayer in 1 Samuel 2, is the joy that runs through it. This is no mother crying as she leaves her child at the bus stop or college for the first time. "My heart exults in the LORD," she sang; "my strength is exalted in the LORD. My mouth derides my enemies, because I rejoice in thy salvation" (1 Sm 2:1). Hannah started from her situation, then moved on to praise God for who he is: Savior. Holy. Solid. Knowledgeable. Judge. One with power over life and death. One who takes down the proud and raises the poor and needy. One who guards his faithful ones and is victorious over his enemies. Everyone, and every situation, is in his hands! With the birth of Samuel, Hannah knew these things to be true beyond a shadow of doubt, from her own experience, and her heart couldn't contain her joy.

Hannah's prayer became a model for praise over the years. There are echoes of it in the psalms, especially Psalm 113. Most notably, Mary borrowed its themes and made them her own in her Magnificat (Lk 1:46–55).

In the time of King David, Elkanah's descendants were among those appointed to minister in song and praise before the tabernacle. Like Hannah's prayer, the prayers they will contribute to the Psalms[3] are marked by gratitude and humility. Psalm 84, which expresses the joy of worship at the Temple, seems to almost be drawn from Hannah's experience as it speaks of the swallow finding a place to lay her young at the Lord's altars (v. 3). "For the LORD God . . . bestows favor and honor," it continues. "No good thing does the LORD withhold from those who walk uprightly" (v. 11). That could have been written by Hannah herself.

As Hannah left Shiloh, the Bible says that Samuel was ministering to the Lord in the presence of Eli—not ministering *with* Eli in the presence of the Lord, which one might expect at his age, and not clinging to his mother's skirts either. He's ministering to the Lord. Where did he learn that? It must have been from Hannah, as Moses got his faith from his mother. Both stories show the value of that early input. Moses went on to be raised in the Egyptian court; Samuel was raised in the tabernacle, but under an ineffectual priest and two wicked, profligate sons. *Yet Samuel heard God there*, and he listened to God's Word and became a great prophet.

How much of that was due to Hannah's influence, not just in his very early years but as she visited at least yearly, bringing clothes, tenderly caring for him, and no doubt praying all the while? Hannah truly was, as Pope John Paul II describes the value of mothers, the one "who is the anchor as the child makes its way along the journey of life."[4] The *Catechism* points out that the family is the "'domestic church' where God's children learn to pray 'as the Church' and to persevere in prayer" (*CCC*, 2685). Surely this was true of Hannah and Elkanah's family. Even at the end of Samuel's life, he was known for unceasing prayer (see 1 Samuel 12:23).

Hannah's faithfulness was rewarded doubly. Each year when they visited Samuel, Eli blessed Hannah and Elkanah and prayed that the Lord would give them children in return for dedicating Samuel to him. They were blessed with three more sons and two daughters, making her like the joyful mother of children in Psalm 113. Hannah returned what God gave her in thanks, and he multiplied the blessing.

CLAIMING HANNAH'S LEGACY: A PATTERN FOR FAITH-FILLED PRAYER

"The prayer of a righteous man has great power in its effects" James writes in his letter to the Jewish Christians of the early Church (Jas 5:16). Clearly that's true of a righteous woman as well! Hannah's prayer was powerful, just as St. Monica's was. What can we learn from her example? What does that kind of effectual prayer look like?

In journalism class I learned that all the important facts of a story can be summed up by answering five *w*'s and two *h*'s: Who? What? When? Where? How? Why? and How much? Hannah's story gives us all of them:

WHOM TO PRAY TO

Hannah goes *to God* in her pain. She could have gone to Elkanah with her problem, or handled it herself—like Sarah, who conscripted Hagar to have a child for her; or Rachel, who demanded a child from Jacob. Hannah, however, went straight to the source of life, certain that God was able to help her. Later, after God gave her a child, she would sing about this (see 1 Samuel 2:5–6). But it's clear by her actions that she already had the confidence of faith.

WHO IS PRAYING

Hannah knew who she was in relationship to God. Three times in one verse she called herself the Lord's "maidservant" (1 Sm 1:11). She didn't make demands or imagine herself to be specially deserving; she only approached God in her need as a servant who depends completely on her master.

WHAT TO PRAY

Hannah poured out what was in her heart. She didn't complain, nag, blame, demand, excuse, or grumble. She simply told God where it hurt and asked if he would give her a son, expressing how grateful she would be. You can take any kind of pain or need to God (see Matthew 6:25–30). He longs for us to ask so he can be there for us, whatever the answer might be. "Cast your burden on the LORD, and he will sustain you; he will never permit the righteous to be moved" (Ps 55:22).

WHEN TO PRAY

Hannah poured out her petition when she was feeling the pain of her distress, getting up after the meal to find an appropriate place for private prayer. And she "continued" to pray, which suggests her prayer was persistent. We too can pray when we feel the need. God doesn't have visiting hours, neither does he sleep. He's there whenever we need him (see Psalm 145:18).

WHERE TO PRAY

Hannah prayed "before the Lord" (1 Sm 1:12) at Shiloh where the ark of the covenant was. This is the first time in the Bible that we read about someone going to a shrine not only to sacrifice or to worship but also to speak to God from the heart. Throughout the Old Testament, although people could and did pray where they were, "the prayer of the People of God flourish[ed] in the shadow of God's dwelling place" (*CCC*, 2578). Then Jesus came as the new Temple, and he left his Spirit to make his home in the temples of our hearts. We still seek his presence for private prayer: whether it's in the "secret" of a prayer closet (Mt 6:6); "where two or three are gathered" (Mt 18:20); or before the Blessed Sacrament, where he is truly present in the Eucharist.

HOW TO PRAY

First, we must pray *from the heart*. Hannah didn't just log her request and move on. She prayed fervently, completely, from the depths of her heart. We can express private prayer on the spot, using our own words, or we can make use of written prayers. Each has its place and value. What is important is that we mean what we say. As the *Catechism* says, "It is the *heart* that prays. If our heart is far from God, the words . . . are in vain" (*CCC*, 2562; emphasis in the original).

We may also pray *with our bodies.* Although Hannah was speaking from her heart, "her lips moved" (1 Sm 1:13). While we may not mouth each word that we pray, if we allow our body to express our prayer—by kneeling, lying prostate, folding our hands or lifting them in supplication, or by speaking or singing—involving our whole being lends our prayer power (see *Catechism*, 2702–2703).

Our inner disposition is also important: we must *pray in faith, trusting God.* As the author of Hebrews says, "Whoever would draw near to God must believe that he exists and that he rewards those who seek him" (Heb 11:6). Hannah knew God was able to help her, believed he would hear and understand her need. He is "a God of knowledge," she sang, who "raises up the poor from the dust" (1 Sm 2:3, 8). She trusted him enough to leave her burden there at the altar, placing the whole problem in his hands to decide as he saw fit. She then left, without knowing God's answer, and worshiped (1 Sm 1:19). That took faith!

While there's no guarantee of a particular result to our prayer, what *is* certain is that "in everything God works for good with those who love him, who are called according to his purpose" (Rom 8:28). Nothing can separate us from his love (Rom 8:35), and he has a way of turning even the blackest situations (think of the Cross!) into occasions of life and glory.

WHY PRAY

In the end, Hannah's plea for a child wasn't about self-gratification. It was more about self-sacrifice. Rachel said to Jacob, "Give me children or I will die." In contrast, Hannah prayed for one son who she could offer back to the Lord.

When our third child was baptized, the priest had us lay him on the altar and offer his life (figuratively, of course) to the Lord. This wasn't a son for us to live through; rather we were accepting stewardship of this child of God's. I think of that day when I read about Hannah's vow (1 Sm 1:11). It's when we seek God's kingdom and delight in him first that our needs and desires are filled.[5]

HOW MUCH TO PRAY

Hannah "continued praying before the Lord" (1 Sm 1:12), even after making her vow. Monica is another example of persistent prayer. She prayed for nearly twenty years! There's no limit on how long or how often we can pray. In fact, St. Paul told the Thessalonians to "pray constantly . . . for this is the will of God in Christ Jesus for you" (1 Thes 5:17–18). Jesus also said that persistence in prayer pays off (see Luke 11:5–10). Hannah's continued prayer opened the door for her request to be answered. As she waited and trusted, she was rewarded.

THEN WHAT?

Because God gave Hannah a son, it's tempting to think about her song of praise, *That's easy for you to say. What if he doesn't give me my desire? What if he doesn't fix my problem?* It's easy to lose trust in God if we focus on the fact that he might say no. Never mind that he has our ultimate good in mind; we'd like to think we know best what will make us happy.

But God isn't a cosmic vending machine; he doesn't simply dispense whatever we want. He's our loving Father who wants our greatest good; above all, he wants us to know and love him. He knows what is best for us, and in what time—and he will also make up to us what is lost because of sin, whether our sin or the pain, brokenness, and injustice that comes from sin in our world. As Christians, we can lift our eyes and set them on eternity where sorrow, pain, and death will have no place and God will wipe away our tears (see Revelations 21:4). In Jesus, pain doesn't have the last word; his love has the last word.

After Hannah's time in prayer, she left in peace and her face was no longer sad. "Transformation of the praying heart is the first response to our petition," according to the *Catechism* (2739). The next morning, Hannah worshipped and went home with no idea of the outcome, only knowing that the Lord had heard. She was able to leave in peace because she had truly given her problem over to God and had faith he would answer in his time and in his way. She found solace in his loving care.

QUESTIONS FOR REFLECTION

- What in Monica's or Hannah's story resonates with you? How have you experienced something similar?
- Recall a time in your life when you asked God for the impossible. What happened? And what did you learn?
- In what situation is God calling you to turn to him today?
- What did you learn from Hannah's story about prayer that you want to put into practice?

ESTHER

GOD HAS CALLED US "FOR SUCH A TIME AS THIS"

[And Mordecai asked Esther,] "Who knows whether you have not come to the kingdom for such a time as this?"

—Esther 4:14

And Esther the queen, seized with deathly anxiety, fled to the Lord.

—Esther 14:1

Thud. Thud. Thud. Thud. A dozen boots stomped in unison as the soldiers who had taken over the neighbor's house did their exercises on the roof. The blare of distant gunfire made it hard to concentrate. Shanghai was preparing to face Mao's army. The American expat missionary families kept their children—my ten-year-old mom and her big sister among them—busy putting on plays.

The next play would be taken from the Old Testament book of Esther, and my mother got the title role. She was beyond excited. All day she'd been practicing her lines and acting royal, to the annoyance of her sister, who told her to stop acting like a princess. "I'm not," she announced. "I'm the queen!" Mom tried on her prettiest dress and put a toy tiara on her head. A magazine cover caught her eye: Princess Elizabeth holding Prince Charles in his long, white christening gown.

"Maybe I *am* a princess," Mom thought to herself. "I'm a daughter of the King of Kings!" She had learned her Sunday school lessons well. A cannon went off in the distance. The Communist army was just four miles away. Mom thought about the soldiers advancing on their city like the Persians prepared to advance on the Jews in Esther's day. "We really might die tonight," she thought, shivering.

Family prayers were sober that evening. As usual, they gathered in a circle. Mother barely paid attention as her siblings prayed one at a time. Her turn was coming and she could think of nothing to add. Queen Esther's words filled her head. *They're going to laugh at me!* she thought. But in the end, she blurted out her lines from the play: "Who knows but we have come for such a time as this? . . . Lord! If we perish, we perish for thee!"

My grandparents always said that those words, quoted by their little girl, my mother Arlita, held them through the long night of bombing. They opened the blackout curtains the next morning on a city in surrender. Buildings all around them had fallen. Bodies and dead horses littered the streets and soldiers slouched away behind a raised white flag. Shanghai had fallen, but the family was alive.

I remember Mother telling that story when I was about the same age as she had been. At school we had air-raid drills so we'd know how to "duck and cover" in case of a Russian nuclear attack. Some families stocked fallout shelters in their backyards. *If I perish, I perish*, I would think, remembering Esther. And I would wonder, as I have many times since then, *If our lives and/or faith were threatened, and I was in a position to do something to save others, would I have the courage? How strong is my faith?*

GETTING THE CONTEXT

Five hundred years after Israel moved into the Promised Land, the territory north of Jerusalem was seized and most of the people were deported to various parts of the Assyrian empire. Before another two centuries passed, the rest of the country was conquered by Babylon. Jerusalem, the Temple, and most of the surrounding area were destroyed and the people were forced into exile. Both times, it was the result of their infidelity to God.

God, however, didn't abandon Israel. He sent word through the prophet Jeremiah to the exiles that they should "seek the welfare of the city where I have sent you into exile, and pray to the LORD on its behalf, for in its welfare you will find your welfare. . . . I will bring you back [home], for I know the plans I have for you, . . . plans for welfare and not for evil, to give you a future and a hope" (Jer 29:7, 11).

That future hope began to be realized seventy years later, when Cyrus, the new Persian king who absorbed most of the Near East (including Israel) into a single empire, allowed the Jews to return to their land. But God continued to be with those who stayed behind. At a time when all Jews throughout the empire were threatened with genocide, it "happened" that a young Jewish orphan had been raised to be queen. It was a providential turn of events that put Esther in the right place at the right time to save her people.

Pope Benedict XVI writes that "it is significant that the woman always figures in Israel's thought and belief, not as priestess, but as prophetess and judge-savior. . . . The powerless one becomes the savior because it is there that the locus for the revelation of God's power is found. After every fall into sin, the woman remains 'mother of life.'"[1]

There are two versions of the book of Esther. The canonical Catholic version follows the Greek Septuagint translation, which includes 107 verses not found in the Hebrew Esther, on which Protestant Bibles are based.[2] In light of Esther's situation—living as a Jewish woman in a land where God isn't recognized, except by the Jews—it's interesting that the Hebrew text never mentions God. Those chapters are like the faithful Jews who lived in exile, who carried God's hidden presence among them. By contrast, the later Greek additions refer to God or the Lord fifty times—making clear what is only suggested or hidden away in the Hebrew, and what is hidden in Esther herself until events call forth the strength of her faith.

ESTHER'S STORY

You can read about Esther in the book of Esther.

ESTHER'S RISE

Susa, the winter residence of the Persian kings, was decked out for a party. Blue and white curtains hung on silver rings from marble pillars; gilded couches sat on a mosaic pavement of precious stones. King Ahasuerus (in Greek, *Artaxerxes*; thought to be Xerxes I) had spent the first years of his reign consolidating his power, and he was ready to celebrate. For six months he showcased his splendor for the nobles and governors of his vast empire to admire. Then he threw a weeklong bash at the palace. Everyone in Susa was invited: the men to the palace courtyard and the women to a separate banquet hosted by Queen Vashti inside.

There seemed to be no end to the golden goblets of wine on offer. Ahasuerus was having a very good time. He decided to show off his beautiful queen and commanded her to appear in her crown. Whether he meant for her to come before the hall of men in *only* her crown is a matter of debate! In any case, she refused. This display of wifely insubordination so angered him that he deposed Vashti and sent letters to every province insisting that "every man be lord in his own house" (Est 1:22).

Living in Susa was a young Jewish girl, Esther. When both of her parents died, her older cousin Mordecai adopted her and raised her as his own. He may have felt a special protectiveness for her because Esther was gorgeous. The Bible describes her as both "beautiful" and "lovely." The first descriptor in Hebrew proclaims her physical beauty. The second is the word used seven times in

Genesis 1 when God calls his creation "good." She was perfection itself; beautiful inside and out.

The name *Esther* is Persian for "star" and is close to the Hebrew word for "hidden." Her Hebrew name, Hadasseh, refers to myrtle, a plant that gives off a lovely fragrance when it's crushed. Together these names describe a girl whose hidden qualities burst forth like a star under pressure. She's an example of how the gift of faith can lie hidden away, "unwrapped" as it were, until circumstances draw it out.

Presumably Mordecai had a Jewish husband in mind for his precious ward. But when Ahasuerus decided it was time to replace his queen, all the loveliest young virgins in the kingdom were brought to his harem for a year of beauty treatments, followed by a night with the king so he could choose the one he wanted. That wasn't as good an opportunity as it might seem. Whether he asked for them again or not, these girls would live out their days in seclusion with the other concubines, cared for but never able to get married or have families of their own. Esther was among the girls of Susa who were taken and put into the custody of Hegai, the eunuch in charge of the harem.

Esther, a girl with no mother or sisters to guide her in the ways of women, was sent to please a king. Maybe her naïveté helped. There she was, surrounded by the most beautiful girls in the kingdom, everyone doing their best to be as ravishing as possible, and even before her year of beauty treatments, she captivated everyone around her. Esther won the favor of Hegai, who gave her seven handpicked maids and moved her into the best part of the harem. When it was her turn to go to the king, she took with her only what Hegai advised. Ahasuerus was entranced. He "loved Esther more than all the women" (Est 2:17) and made her his queen.

Without her God-given looks, Esther would never have captured the king. It's to her credit that in the end, rather than using that beauty to save herself, she would risk it to save her people. And that is where her true beauty lay.

MORDECAI'S MISSION

Outside the harem, life continued as usual. Mordecai served in the king's court and sat at the king's gate, where business was done. One day he overheard a plot against the king and told it to Esther, who passed his warning to the king. The villains were hanged and the incident recorded in the king's books. Later, the king promoted a man named Haman to his second in command and ordered everyone to bow in Haman's presence. Mordecai, a devoted Jew who would bow only before God, refused. Haman was so incensed that he determined to destroy all the Jewish people.

Haman induced Ahasuerus to issue a decree that on a certain day every Jewish man, woman, and child in the kingdom be destroyed "without pity or mercy" (Est 13:6). He offered to make an enormous donation if the law was passed, and soon the decree went out to all the land. "The king and Haman sat down to drink; but the city of Susa was perplexed" (Est 3:15).

News reached Esther that Mordecai was going about the city wailing in sackcloth and ashes. Distressed at the news, she sent him clothes to replace the sackcloth. When he refused them, she sent an attendant to find out what was wrong. Apparently the edict, which had circulated throughout the entire kingdom, had not penetrated the walls of the harem. Mordecai sent her a copy of the decree and pled with her to pray and to intercede with the king of their behalf.

Esther was at a crossroads. After six years, the palace had become her world. She had told no one there that she was a Jew. Did she remember her heritage? Would she take advantage of her position to hide and save her skin, or would she stand up and help her people? Her answer, which she shared with one her attendants, reflected ambivalence and fear: "The king hasn't asked to see me in a month," she said, "and it's against the law to approach him uninvited. Anyone who does is killed—unless the king holds out his royal scepter; but there's no guarantee of that" (see Esther 4:11).

Mordecai told Esther not to think she'd be saved just because she's queen: "For if you keep silence at such a time as this, relief and deliverance will rise for the Jews from another quarter, but you and your father's house will perish. And who knows whether you have not come to the kingdom for such a time as this?" (Est 4:14).

For such a time as this! Was it coincidence that she was made queen, or was she part of God's plan to save? Like their ancestor Joseph, who was sold into Egyptian slavery only to be raised to a position of power where he could save God's people from famine,[3] Esther wasn't raised just for her own good, and definitely not just to be an ornament on the arm of the king; she was raised "for such a time as this."

Mordecai's reminder of God's providence had its effect: Esther chose her people. She had Mordecai ask all the Jews of Susa to join her and her maids in a three-day fast.[4] "Then I will go to the king, though it is against the law; and if I perish, I perish" (Est 4:16), she said.

ESTHER'S PRAYER

The details of Esther's fast and the words of her prayer are recorded in the Greek additions to the text, which fall between Esther 4 and 5 in the Catholic Bible. Like Hannah, Esther poured her heart out before the One she knew could help. Like Judith, whom we will meet next, Esther prayed for courage and "eloquent speech"—not to deceive the king but to persuade him. She asked God to turn the king's heart against Haman and to save her people. She prayed in spite of her fear, or maybe because of it, and was given the courage she needed. "And Esther, the queen, seized with deathly anxiety, fled to the Lord. . . . 'Help me, who am alone and have no helper but thee, O Lord. . . . And save me from my fear!'" (Est 14:1, 14, 19).

Esther replaced her splendid clothes and jewels with sackcloth, ashes, and dung. She let her hair go wild. She fasted and she prayed. Then on the third day, she emerged from prayer with a plan. She cleaned herself up and approached the king. "Majestically adorned, after invoking the aid of the all-seeing God and Savior, . . . she was radiant with perfect beauty . . . but her heart was frozen with fear. . . . She stood before the king" (Est 15:2, 5, 6). God changed the king's heart from anger to concern for Esther (see Esther 15:8), so that he put himself at her disposal.

Notice that courage is not the absence of fear. (I wonder, can you even have courage if you're not afraid?) Esther was terrified, yet she acted in holy boldness. Where did that come from? Read her prayer and you will see. Like Rahab, Esther knew who God is. She knew his character. She knew what he had done for them in the past. She knew what he had promised and that he was greater than any earthly king. Esther's plea sprang out of her faith. Like Esther, when we're afraid, we can take recourse in God who gives courage.

THE JEWS ARE SAVED

We've seen God raise women to save his people through prophecy and military leadership; now we see how Esther operated from the feminine strengths of hospitality and sensitivity. She had already shown she knew how to please the king. It seems she understood the enemy, Haman, as well. Twice she was received into the king's presence. Twice she was offered up to half the kingdom, and both times she ignored the offer. All she asked was that the king and Haman come to a dinner that she would prepare for them. Esther prudently created a setting in which the king would want to please her and in which she could be heard.

Pope John Paul II writes that true beauty is revealed when "ordinary women . . . reveal the gift of their womanhood by placing themselves at the service of others . . . in their greatness and limitations."[5]

That's true in everyday ways as much as it is in times like Esther's. I learned it from the smile a high school senior gave me one day when I was a lonely, awkward freshman. She was beautiful, popular—something I would never be in school. She could have used her popularity to put me down. Instead, she gave me value with her smile. That smile also gave me strength and purpose. From then on, I looked for people to be kind to. She may have no idea what she did with that glance, but with it she showed her true beauty.

Esther exemplifies that principle as well. God gifted her with beauty and grace that could capture a king's heart and put her in a position to use it. She could have shut her eyes to what was happening outside and focused on her jewels and finery. She could have asked for half the kingdom. But instead she offered to fix a simple dinner.

Haman was elated by that honor. But not even the thought of dinner with the queen made up for the dishonor he felt when Mordecai didn't bow. He decided to have Mordecai hanged and ordered gallows built for the purpose; only then could he enjoy Esther's dinner in peace.

That night, a fit of insomnia sent the king to his book of deeds, where he read about the good turn Mordecai did in exposing the plot against him. Realizing he had never properly honored him, Ahasuerus asked Haman (who had come to the palace to ask to hang Mordecai) what he should do to honor someone worthy. Haman, imagining the glory would be shown to himself, suggested that the man be robed in splendor and crowned and led by a prince around the city on a royal horse. In a twist of poetic justice, the king commanded Haman to honor Mordecai publicly in the way he had described. It was a subdued and humiliated Haman who presented himself at the queen's second banquet.

Things got worse for Haman when Ahasuerus asked Esther at that dinner what he could do for her. This time, she pleaded for her life and the life of her people. When the king learned that Haman was responsible for her plight, he left in a rage, returning to see Haman lying on the queen's couch where he was begging for mercy (Est 7:8). Mistaking that for assault, and learning of the gallows he'd built for Mordecai, the king sent Haman out to be hanged.

Esther dared once more to go before the king. When he held out his scepter to receive her, she begged him to revoke his order against the Jews. Signed orders couldn't be undone, so he gave her authority to write something new. She and Mordecai had letters sent out in the king's name allowing the Jews to defend themselves on the day of the attack and to destroy those who attacked them—which they did. Esther's people were saved!

CLAIMING ESTHER'S LEGACY: GOD EQUIPS US FOR THE WORK HE GIVES US

I'm a big fan of God's providence: the ways by which God guides us with wisdom and love to our ultimate end; his "plan of sheer goodness" to invite us to never-ending blessing in heaven (see *Catechism*, 1). Queen or no queen, I have a royal destiny. As my mother realized all those years ago, no matter what I look like, where I live, or how much I have now, I *am* a princess. I am a daughter of the King of Kings!

That's true of every one of us who belong to God. We are daughters of the King, born "for such a time as this." From where we sit, "this" might look like a palace or the inside of a harem or a drab place of exile. Being born for "this" doesn't mean "this" is our ultimate end. It means we're uniquely positioned with our particular gifts, experiences, abilities, and limitations to do something to further God's kingdom *here*—in this place, at this time, and among these people. Sometimes if we lift up our eyes from our troubles, we'll see God's hand outstretched to us. *I'm going this way. Are you coming?* Esther took his hand, as afraid as she was, and that made all the difference. She could have been just another forgotten pretty face with lovely things to wear. Instead, she saved her people.

Of course, not everyone's called to do something that dramatic. But why not me? I have it in me to be a queen . . . don't I? St. Thérèse of Lisieux struggled with the question of why God doesn't raise everyone to the same height of glory, and God invited her to look at his creation. Lilies may stand regally above the rest of the flowers, she realized, but in no way do they take away from the sweetness of violets or the columbine's wild beauty. God loves the simple and delights in the daisy as much as the rose. "And just as in nature all the seasons are arranged in such a way as to make the humblest daisy bloom on a set day, in the same way," she writes, "everything works out for the good of each soul."[6]

St. Thérèse also learned that "all souls cannot be the same, that it is necessary there be different types in order to honor each of God's perfections in a particular way."[7] And because God loves the simple and the small, he often raises unlikely people to do his work. A young, orphaned Jewish girl, however pretty she was, wasn't likely to become queen of the most powerful empire on earth. Neither was it likely that she would save her people from genocide! Even when she was queen, she had no power to speak of. What she did have was access to the Most High God. She fasted. She prayed. She clung to what she knew to be true about God. She asked for wisdom, she went out on a limb, she did the simple things that she could do. And then she let God work.

QUESTIONS FOR REFLECTION

- How does Arlita's story show you how God provides for his children? How have you experienced that in your own life?
- What about Esther's courageous story resonates with you? When have you experienced what it feels like to right a grievous wrong, to advocate for justice?
- How is God calling you out of your comfort zone today?
- What did you learn from this chapter that might strengthen your courage?

JUDITH

GOD CREATED OUR BEAUTY FOR GOOD

But the Lord Almighty has foiled [Israel's
    enemy]
    by the hand of a woman. . . .
Judith the daughter of Merari undid him
    with the beauty of her countenance.
                                    —Judith 16:6, 7

You [Judith] are blessed by the Most High
God above all women on earth; and blessed
be the Lord God, who . . . has guided you to
strike the head of the leader of our enemies.
                                    —Judith 13:18

The photo in my hand is from 1973. Arthur and his wife Avonna
Lee are dressed to celebrate: he in a suit, she in a floor-length hand-
loomed and beaded skirt they purchased on a trip to South Africa.
At her waist is a lovely corsage. Both of them are smiling; it's their
wedding anniversary and she looks radiant.

Avonna Lee, my mother's cousin, is one of those women whose
beauty can't be explained by her features alone. Her face is lovely
to look at, true; but what you notice is the light that spills out and
envelops you when you're with her. She's an accomplished artist,
and that same light suffuses her paintings. She has spent a lifetime

seeking the beauty of God's holiness. It shows in everything she is and does.

Not long ago, Avonna Lee gave me the skirt she wore in that picture. It's in perfect condition. And it fits! I'm proud to wear it—not just because it's lovely but also because I feel as though in putting it on, I'm clothing myself with some of her style and spirit.

The year that photo was taken, Arthur was commissioned by the World Council of Churches to help find out what was going on in South Africa under apartheid. The country was closed to reporters, but rumors were filtering out: forced segregation; whole villages bulldozed; people jailed on trumped-up charges, tortured, killed. Some of the pastors had written testimonials for Arthur to smuggle back. At the same time, Avonna Lee had an appointment with the national museum of South Africa. Along with several of her paintings, she brought a small, hidden camera to take pictures of injustices they saw in the country.

She tells how afraid she was when they arrived in South Africa and were questioned by the Special Branch, part of the police force that was charged with rooting out anti-apartheid activities. She did her best to look relaxed and put on a friendly, trusting smile. The officers looked at her passport photo, then at her. She looked up and forced herself to sparkle. "Look at her blue eyes," one of them said. "She's alright, you can let her through." A small miracle! But she learned then that whatever it was that she had in her eyes and her smile, it could keep the men from looking further.

For the rest of their stay in South Africa, Avonna Lee and Arthur were followed everywhere. Their rooms were bugged. They had to act completely innocent and natural, even when they were sweating with fear, so as not to draw attention to themselves or put the people they met in danger. Often they had to split up, not knowing if the other was safe until nightfall when they returned to the hotel. Every morning, Avonna Lee thought carefully about what she would wear and how to fix her hair: not in order to seduce but to disarm, to cast an "invisibility cloak" over what she was doing. Then she prayed for protection and guidance. "When I needed help,

I'd be led by God to do or say something clever," she said. She didn't always understand the words she was given, but later they'd turn out to be providential. The Lord protected them both.

As she packed for the flight home, Avonna Lee carefully hid the letters, photos, and rolls of film. She tucked them in the soles of their shoes and inside her bras where she didn't think anyone would look; she slid them down the front of her skirt. Arthur got safely on the plane but they held her back. "Who are you?" "Why were you here?" "What are you doing?"—the questions kept coming and she was all alone. Then one officer raised his eyebrows as if to say, *Get a load of her.* She didn't realize it but she had pushed her big dark sunglasses up on top of her head. "Oh—that Jackie Kennedy look!" said the other man. "Yes, she's an artist," they laughed. They stopped asking questions and let her go.

As I think of those men being thrown off their game by sparkling blue eyes and a pair of mod sunglasses—and, no doubt, by her aura of virtue and trustworthiness—I think of Judith. She's the biblical heroine who used her beauty to disarm a powerful enemy who was poised to destroy her city, then killed him. I've never been quite comfortable with Judith. (Spoiler alert: What kind of woman cuts off a man's head and carries it home in her bag! Really?) But maybe it's time to take another look.

GETTING THE CONTEXT

When I was a kid, we spent rainy days play-acting David and Goliath, using the dialog we learned from 1 Samuel 17, in a box my mom set up on the kitchen table. I'd form a hill of sand on each side of a "stream" of foil to make a battlefield for the Israelites (a handful of green army men) versus Goliath (a menacing G.I. Joe). One of my brothers would move little David onto the field and shout, "For who is this uncircumcised Philistine, that he should defy the armies of the living God?" Goliath (another brother) would roar back, "Am I a dog, that you [fight] me with sticks?" Then the response: "You might have a spear, but I come in the name of God. Prepare to die!" (Okay, we played with the words a little.) And a tiny green man would hurl something at Goliath, knock him down, and chop off his head with the soldier's plastic gun.

Unfortunately, our Protestant Bible didn't have the book of Judith to inspire our dramatic performances.[1] Yet if someone had recounted the story to us, we would have found that Judith's story (which is found in Catholic Bibles) was much like David's. A fearsome enemy challenges Israel and defies both the people and their God. Everyone is terrified. Then the last person you'd expect steps out in faith and crushes the "giant," humiliating him and using the enemy's own sword to cut off his head. Israel is saved not by might but by faith in the living God.

Whether the story of Judith is based on an actual event isn't known. Obvious historical "mistakes"—like the identification of King Nebuchadnezzar with Assyria instead of Babylon in Judith 1:1—call that into question. It seems that the author drew on names and events that were well known to his audience in order to evoke a massive threat. (The real Nebuchadnezzar, king of Babylon, destroyed Jerusalem and exiled the southern kingdom in 587 BC, and Assyria exiled the northern tribes over a century before that.) The net effect is a quasi-historical novel that packs a strong message that God is much bigger than any giant, and no enemy, however strong, can defeat Israel if they stay true to God. Even someone who appears weak—a widow such as Judith, for example, or a weak nation such as Israel under the Greeks—can be an instrument of victory because it's God's power, not military might, that overcomes.

Judith means "Jewess" or, more literally, "woman of Judea"—which comes, in turn, from the name *Judah*, which means "praise." It's a fitting name for a representational heroine. Judith represents all the Jewish people in the ideal. They are the people of God who is "enthroned on [their] praises" (Ps 22:3).

Read in the context of the rest of the Bible, we've met Judith's type before in the sense of a woman representing Israel. Ezekiel describes how God rescued Israel as an infant, gave her beautiful clothing and jewels, and made her his bride (see Ezekiel 16). But she used her beauty to seduce other lovers: gods and nations she showered with the riches and blessings God had given her.

In Hosea, we read that God had Hosea marry a prostitute to show Israel how God loved them in spite of their betrayal. When Hosea's wife abandoned him, he sent her into the desert where, stripped of her blessings, she could remember his love and return. Israel didn't heed the warning, and it happened to them: they were taken into exile by the nations they "seduced."

When Judith was written, the Jewish people had returned to the Lord and were back in their land. They were sadder but wiser, wanting to serve only God. But the other nations were circling again. They desired her beauty and resources for themselves. How would the Jews use what they'd been given this time? Would they offer themselves to the invaders or would they trust and wait on God? Their hope, suggests the book, lies in being who they are—the beautiful, holy spouse of the Most High God—and relying on him.

JUDITH'S STORY

You can read about Judith in the book of Judith.

The first half of Judith's book isn't about her at all. A full seven chapters are given to explaining the full horror of the political situation. King Nebuchadnezzar had sent his general Holofernes on the warpath. The army set out, slaughtering whole towns and ravaging everything in its path.

As the book of Judith tells it, the Jews had only recently returned from exile in Babylon. That experience had cured them of wanting to trust in other nations and false gods. They had just rebuilt their Temple. They weren't about to cede it to Gentiles again. They blocked the passes in the hills, prepared for war, and prayed to God with all their might.

Holofernes was furious that this gnat of a nation would dare to resist. The Ammonite leader Achior warned him that, based on past experience, Israel couldn't be defeated unless they sinned against their God. Holofernes took this as an affront against his king—"Who is God except Nebuchadnezzar?" he bellowed (Jdt 6:2)—and sent Achior, bound hand and foot, to await his fate in Bethulia, a tiny mountain town located at the entry to Judea. Holofernes brought out a massive force against them. He cut off their water supply and waited for Bethulia to surrender to famine and slaughter.

A month later, there wasn't enough water in the city to last a single day. Children were crying; women and young men were fainting in the streets. Certain that God had sold them into the hands of their enemies, the people pressed their rulers to surrender. Uzziah, chief among the governors, begged them to hold out for another five days. "If God doesn't save us by then, I'll surrender," he swore. The chapter closes with, "And they were greatly depressed in the city" (Jdt 7:32). No kidding! The scene was set for our heroine to act.

JUDITH'S PLEA

Judith might have been the only person in Bethulia not wailing in the streets or begging to surrender. She was at home, praying as usual in a tent she set up on her roof. This daily habit seems to have given her a perspective the others had lost.

Judith seems too good to be true: drop-dead gorgeous, wealthy, with a pedigree of no less than sixteen ancestral names tracing her back to Jacob. She was also God-fearing and virtuous. With the help of a trusted maid, she maintained the estate left her by her late husband. Although she was a widow, she wasn't looking for another husband. While many women blessed with beauty, brains, and wealth might be resented, no one spoke against Judith because they knew of her total devotion to God (see Judith 8:8). She had the respect of the entire community.

When word came to Judith that Uzziah had sworn to surrender, she sent her maid to summon the elders. "Listen to me, rulers of the people of Bethulia!" she said (Jdt 8:11). "What you've done is not right," she told them. "Who are you to put God to the test, promising to surrender us to our enemies if he doesn't help in so many days? He's not someone you can threaten or force to do something. Don't make him mad!" (see Judith 8:11, 12–14).

Judith's plea was magnificent, full of common sense, righteous anger, and faith. Bethulia's ancestors may have run after idols, but this generation had not. Yahweh was their God and they should hope in him alone. She reminded the elders that if they were to let the enemy past, all Judea would fall. "Let us set an example to our brethren," she pleaded, "for their lives depend upon us. . . . In spite of everything let us give thanks to the Lord our God, who is putting us to the test as he did our forefathers" (Jdt 8:24, 25).

I love that last sentence: "In spite of everything let us give thanks to the Lord." St. Paul writes something like that in 1 Thessalonians 5:18: "Give thanks in all circumstances; for this is the will of God in Christ Jesus for you." Whether that means the circumstances are his will or that his will is for me to give thanks, the upshot is the same: in whatever circumstance we find ourselves, the Lord wants us to turn our attention to him and give thanks. He is the one who is able to help; he is the one who will judge, who will reward, who will make all things well. A thankful heart restores perspective to the soul and helps us to trust.

Uzziah praised Judith's insight and wisdom, but held to his oath. "Pray for us," he said, "and the Lord will answer you and send us rain" (see Judith 8:31).

JUDITH'S PLAN

That's not the answer Judith had hoped for. "Listen to me" (Jdt 8:32), she said again. "I'm going to do something that will go down in history. Don't ask me what. But know that within the next five days, before the date you have set for surrender, the Lord will deliver Israel through me" (see Judith 8:32–33).

Then she fell on her face and cried out to God.

I love this woman. She was so certain of God that she was ready to risk her life so he could act. She said:

> Behold their pride, and . . . give to me, a widow, the
> strength to do what I plan. By the deceit of my lips strike
> down the . . . prince with his servant; crush their arro-
> gance by the hand of a woman.[2]
>
> For thy power depends not upon numbers, nor thy
> might upon men of strength. . . . Cause thy whole nation
> and every tribe to know and understand that thou art
> God, the God of all power and might, and that there
> is no other who protects the people of Israel but thou
> alone! (Jdt 9:9–11, 14)

Judith's plan was bold. She armed herself with the gifts God
gave her: beauty and wit. She put on her party clothes and jewels
and put a tiara in her hair, making herself "very beautiful, to entice
the eyes of all men who might see her" (Jdt 10:4). The Latin Vulgate
adds, "All this dressing up did not proceed from sensuality, but
from virtue: and therefore the Lord increased this her beauty, so
that she appeared to all men's eyes incomparably lovely."[3] Beauty
is a gift—an essentially feminine gift that reflects in a unique way
the beauty of God's holiness, goodness, and love, like the masculine gift of strength reflects his power and majesty. Judith's beauty
was part of God's plan to free his people. Her feminine gifts would
be as effective against the enemy as David's sling and stones were
against Goliath.

Judith went with her maid to meet the elders at the gate. They
were astounded by her appearance and blessed her. Judith worshipped God and headed out to meet Holofernes, all eyes on her
as she went.

Her arrival at the enemy camp caused quite a stir. You'd expect
her to have been eaten alive (figuratively speaking). But a hundred men gave Judith an armed escort to their leader, who jumped
up from under his jeweled canopy to marvel at her beauty. Not
only was she stunning but she also offered him a sure way to take
Bethulia. It was true, she said, that no one could overcome them
unless they sinned against God. But they were about to do just that.
The lack of food and water was tempting them to consume things

consecrated to God, which so offended her that she fled and was now appealing to Holofernes. She told him, "God has sent me to accomplish with you things that will astonish the whole world" (Jdt 11:16). That was true! But not in the way he thought. Holofernes loved her plan: she would go into the valley each night to worship, and when God told her the people had sinned, she would report back and he'd go in and conquer.

For three days Judith stayed in her tent, going out only at night with her maid to bathe at the spring and pray for guidance. At all times her behavior was chaste. On the fourth day, Holofernes held a private banquet for his guest. Some women might have used their beauty to seduce him and build their own power. But Judith turned down his offers. God gave her clever words to use so that the general heard what he wanted to hear. Blinded by her beauty, he underestimated her wisdom. And he was so excited by what he hoped would follow the meal that he "drank a great quantity of wine, much more than he had ever drunk in any one day since he was born" (Jdt 12:20). Needless to say, by the time his servants shut them in for the night, he had passed out cold on the bed.

JUDITH'S TRIUMPH

It was the moment Judith had been waiting for. She prayed twice for God's help and strength, then took Holofernes's sword down from the wall. She got a grip on his hair and with two strikes cut off his head. She took the jeweled canopy from the bed as proof of who he was, and with the head safely stowed in their food bag, she went with her maid as usual into the night.

This time they passed through the valley and up the mountain to Bethulia. Judith gave a triumphant shout to the watchmen and everyone came running. As she showed them the evidence that the dreaded general was dead, she praised God for being with his people, destroying their enemy (by a woman, no less!), and protecting her virtue in the process. Uzziah responded with words that recall Deborah's blessing of Jael and that are reflected years later in the angel's words to Mary at the annunciation: "O daughter, you are

blessed by the Most High God above all women on earth; and blessed be the Lord God, who created the heavens and the earth, who
has guided you to strike the head of the leader of our enemies. Your
hope will never depart from the hearts of men, as they remember
the power of God" (Jdt 13:18–19).

Judith knew the job wasn't done. She told the people to hang
Holofernes's head on the city wall and gather an army as though
they were about to attack. She predicted that the Assyrians would
flee when they discovered their captain was dead, which is exactly
what happened. "One Hebrew woman has brought disgrace upon
the house of King Nebuchadnezzar!" wailed the steward from his
tent. "For look, here is Holofernes lying on the ground, and his head
is not on him!" (Jdt 14:18). The Assyrian army rushed out and the
men of Israel chased them down to their death.

Judith took her tambourine and led the women in a great victory dance and song of thanksgiving and praise to God, and the men
followed behind. The celebration ended in worship at the Temple,
where Judith devoted the plunder she was given to the Lord. Her
fame grew but she turned down all offers of marriage, remaining
a widow to the end of her very long life. "And no one ever again
spread terror among the people of Israel in the days of Judith, or
for a long time after her death" (Jdt 16:25). Such is the heritage of
this woman who put her faith in God.

CLAIMING JUDITH'S LEGACY:
BE WHO YOU'RE
CREATED TO BE

Ah, Judith.

She strikes different women in different ways. "I. Love. Judith!"
is something I hear a lot when I mention her. "She's such a badass,"
I've heard, or "She's fierce!"—admiring her courage and strength.
Especially, in the #MeToo era, her bold independence (and let's

be honest, the way she utterly defeats Holofernes) makes her an attractive role model and gives her street cred. Judith is smart and clear-headed, and she gets the job done without relying on men.

Judith isn't afraid of her beauty. It never makes her a plaything or victim. She knows what she has and she's not afraid to use it. For the same reason, some people don't like her at all. Beauty is so often used to seduce or to hurt that some want it hidden. It's such a potent weapon, the argument goes, that like a gun it should be locked away. As it says in Sirach 36:27, "A woman's beauty lights up a man's face, and there is nothing he desires more" (NRSV). The author of Song of Solomon begged his love not to look at him, as he found her beauty as terrible as an advancing army (6:4–5).

Certainly beauty can be misused. But all beauty points to God, and its power can be used for good. For example, men who fought with Joan of Arc spoke of her beauty and the passionate-yet-chaste love she inspired in them that made them willing to face death in battle.[4] Something of the sort may have been what motivated Barak and others who fought willingly for Deborah in Judges 4. And Avonna Lee's experience showed me how disarming beauty can be when we're facing an enemy.

In all of those cases, it was the inner beauty of virtue that gave the outer appearance power for good. Which is why it's important that Judith is beautiful *and* good. "Pretty is as pretty does," my mother used to say to me. Let's not relegate beauty to the mean girls and wicked stepmothers or even to the victims of the world. Remember Genesis 1? God saw it was "good"—the Hebrew also means "beautiful." Good nature and beautiful appearance went hand in hand then, reflecting God's goodness and the beauty of his holiness. Just because the Fall ripped the two things apart and beauty can be misused doesn't mean they can't go together. It's not true that goodness comes only in plain and ugly packages, or that beauty has to hide a rotten core.

Judith is the whole package. Which is why we might admire her but can't relate to her. We prefer our heroes flawed. It helps us think we can be like them. But that's setting our sights too low. We're made for more than "almost beautiful" or "sometimes good."

On one hand, Judith is none of us. She is an ideal, after all. But on the other hand, she is all of us. In her beauty, holiness, and humility, and by the fact that she isn't tempted by the enemy but cuts off his head, she prefigures Mary and ultimately the victorious Church. We're part of that Church. St. Paul describes Jesus as presenting the Church to himself like a bride "in splendor, without spot or wrinkle . . . that she might be holy and without blemish" (Eph 5:27). The Church is blessed with beauty and fine gifts and "the powers of death shall not prevail against it" (Mt 16:18).

Judith is what God made you and me to be: beautiful in holiness and strong in him. In her prayerful humility, she saw herself as God made her. She received his gift of beauty, didn't downplay it but acted out of it and allowed him to work through it.

In the end, beauty isn't measured by physical features but by our likeness to the One in whose image we're created. So do we measure ourselves against others, then manipulate our beauty to form our own image? Or do we see ourselves as God sees us and allow him to mold us into his likeness?

God wants to make us "good" in the Genesis 1 sense of the word. Not a goody-two-shoes, afraid-to-do-anything-wrong sort of good. A beautiful, magnificent good that's terrible in its splendor. Like the ideal that is Judith. Like Mary to whom Judith points, who embodies that ideal woman. Like Jesus who won the victory, whom we will be like one day when we see him as he is (see 1 John 3:2).

AN INVITATION

God's hand is outstretched in love toward you.

Are you coming? he asks.

He knows you're a flawed daughter of Eve. But he created you to be beautiful and chose you to be bride of his Son. Your story isn't over.

You may struggle, like Sarah, to follow when you can't see the way. Like Leah or Rachel, your heart might ache for what you can't have. You may have been caught out in your imperfection, like Miriam, or like Rahab you could be facing a storm. Maybe, like Deborah, those around you aren't leading; or like Ruth, you might have lost all you had. You may be drowning in sorrow like Hannah or trapped in Esther's golden cage or even facing death.

"Arise, my love, my fair one, and come away" (Sg 2:10), he calls.

Take his hand and follow. He sees you like Judith. Become who you are!

QUESTIONS FOR REFLECTION

- What about Avonna Lee's or Judith's story resonates with you?
- How has your beauty been a source of inspiration—or temptation?
- In what particular way is God calling you to grow in true beauty today?
- What did you learn from this chapter that might help you to act confidently in the gifts you've been given?

DAUGHTER OF GOD, BE A MOTHER OF FAITH!

> [W]hat the virgin Eve had bound fast through unbelief, this did the virgin Mary set free through faith.
>
> —St. Irenaeus of Lyon

Mary, like Eve, woke up to love.

At the end of her life on earth, the Church teaches, Mary was taken body and soul into heaven and reunited with her beloved Son. What a wonderful reunion that must have been! Artists throughout the centuries have tried to capture the moment.

My favorite depiction is in the crypt below the Church of the Dormition on Mount Zion, in Jerusalem. At the center of a large room lies a life-sized statue of Mary, lying as though asleep on a marble bier. Six columns rise around her and support a domed roof punctuated by mosaic "windows" into heaven. Dominating the center of the dome, Jesus leans over his mother, his arms held out either in prayer or welcome or both. A small smile lights his face as he waits for Mary to rise. Around him stands a royal welcoming committee of great Old Testament women:

- Eve, with the serpent safely behind her, raises a hand of refusal to the forbidden fruit as she looks down on the "new Eve" sleeping below.

- Miriam looks to heaven as she taps out a rhythm on her tambourine, perhaps leading a choir of angels in song.
- Jael grips a tent peg in one hand, a mallet in the other, ready to defend her people.
- Judith lifts the head of Holofernes as if to say, "The battle's over!"
- Ruth holds a sheaf of wheat in one arm while her other hand moves to her breast, perhaps indicating the royal children—including Jesus—who come from her line.
- Esther stands in her queenly robes, holding a scepter aloft as she greets the new queen of heaven who will advocate on our behalf.

What was it like for these women to meet Mary? It must have been like Moses and Elijah meeting Jesus at the Transfiguration and talking about his "exodus" that he'll accomplish in Jerusalem (Lk 9:28–31). Everything those men prefigured, the Law and the Prophets, was reborn in a new and definitive way in Jesus Christ. Similarly, everything these women yearned and strived for, seeing and greeting it from afar, as Hebrews 11:13 puts it, came about in Mary and her Son.

In my imagination, the women—these six and the others we have met—greet Mary even before she makes it to the heavenly throne room. They dress her in beautiful robes and start talking as they take her to the banquet. About what she has accomplished, about what Jesus is doing, and about the people who will follow. Because everything that Mary is anticipates what we will be as members of the Church in heaven. We (I hope!) will be the Body of Christ and her children, those who "keep the commandments of God and bear testimony to Jesus" (Rv 12:17). Like her, we'll live, body and soul, in heaven. Like her, we will reign.

The women of the Word we have met in this book are part of the great "cloud of witnesses" that Hebrews 12:1 says surrounds us as we run toward the finish line. That they prefigure Mary doesn't mean we should discard them. In the same way that men such as Adam, Abraham, Moses, and David help us understand Jesus and what it means to have faith, these women prepare for and help us understand the role of Mary in salvation. They also show us the dignity of motherhood and its place in God's plan; they help us deal with things such as waiting, barrenness, and sorrow; the importance of praise and obedience; and how to fight and deal with fear.

Ultimately these women point to Mary whose yes to God's call was as deadly to the serpent as Judith's sword was to Holofernes. In my mind's eye, I see them leaning out of heaven's door behind the outstretched hand of Christ. *Are you coming?* These women are cheering us on, encouraging us to say yes!

They are our mothers in faith.

MARY SHOWS THE WAY

On a Marian pilgrimage I helped lead in the Holy Land, one of my uncles came along. "Are you sure you want to go," I asked, "given that you have trouble with Catholic beliefs about Mary?" He did indeed.

On the last day, he shared his experience with the group. Sitting in the Church of Mary's Tomb at the foot of the Mount of Olives, he'd watched as a woman shuffled up to a large painting of Mary that hung at the back of the hall behind the tomb. She gazed at it a moment, then moved close and lay her head against the Blessed Mother's breast for a full minute or more, before walking away. "I realized then," he said, "what it means that Mary's a mother!" He went on to speak of how moved he had been throughout the trip, watching one of the pilgrims. That woman, also named Mary, had brought her grown daughters along to help them meet Jesus in a new way.

This is what Mary does as our mother, is it not? Along with interceding on our behalf, she always takes us to Jesus. As a new Catholic, I had it backward. I had to ask Jesus to take me to his mother. And I'll admit, I didn't think I needed her. If I thought about Mary, which wasn't often, I thought of her more as a statue or a set of doctrines than a person.

What my uncle perceived in a flash took me years to realize. It began with a sense I had of her presence when a Rosary was prayed before Mass. More subtly, the women I love in the Bible began to point me in her direction. Then studying the annunciation, I saw how God reached out to Mary and I realized she's the quintessential "woman of the Word." The way she listened to the Word of God . . . received it in her heart . . . pondered it . . . and allowed it to take root in her and grow until she, herself, gave him flesh! I wanted then to sit at Mary's feet and learn to take God's hand and be a woman of the Word—a mother of the Word—myself. All I know of faith is packed into her life and her example. I am grateful to each woman of the Word—the women in the Bible—who prepared the way for her. And I am grateful to each woman of the Word—those women in my life who loved and lived the Word before me, who listened to it and followed—for paving the way of faith.

TREASURING OUR LEGACY AND PASSING IT ON

As I sifted through the stories that are part of my heritage, I couldn't shake the sense that I've been entrusted with something precious. These pearls of witness, like my grandmother's pearls I'll inherit someday, weren't treasured, polished, and passed down only to end with me. With this book I entrust them to you. There's a pearl for each of the biblical women, each with its own color and luster. There are other pearls for Great-Grandma Jennie; for Grandmas Helen and Grace; for my mother, Aunt Betty, and Avonna Lee. There's a pearl for St. Monica. And my own little seed pearls are woven throughout.

I know that you have a string of pearls too. A necklace of faith. Think for a moment: What women in your life faced doubt and emptiness, danger and sorrow, with faith—and passed on how God helped them through? Who taught you your prayers? Who encouraged you to be who you are? Who showed you your beauty, or walked with you when times were hard? Who taught you how to say yes?

Treasure those pearls; tie them together and add some of your own. If your string is empty, start now. Wrap that nacre of forgiveness around the problems in your life. Pour love into the need of others. And when God asks, *Are you coming?* take his hand—and your tambourine—and go forward in faith and praise!

ACKNOWLEDGMENTS

What began as a simple book about some of the women of the Old Testament took on a life of its own as I spent time with Eve and Sarah, Rachel and Leah, and the others and began remembering some of the women in my own life. I am deeply grateful to Ave Maria Press, particularly publisher Tom Grady for believing in me and for giving me time and space to go where these biblical ladies took me. In addition, the book would not exist in any form without the persistent support and encouragement of Heidi Saxton. Thank you for your endless patience, your gracious editing and spot-on insights, and your friendship over the years.

Thank you also to the Ave team: Karey Circosta, Kristen Bonelli, Stephanie Sibal, Amber Elder, Susana Kelly, and Emily Wickland: every author should have you in their corner as you have been in mine. I think especially of the way the whole editorial team pulled together to find just the right title, faced with a complex and shifting focus. When you came up with this one, the whole thing fell into place.

Ten chapters aren't nearly enough to speak of all the women who have mothered me in faith and who in some way inspired this book. Those I wrote about—my grandmothers and great-grandmother, Mom, Avonna Lee, and Aunt Betty—I owe so much. I am especially grateful to those who are still with me: Mom and Avonna Lee, thank you for your generous love and for letting me tell some of your stories. That I didn't mention others (and maybe some would rather I didn't!) doesn't mean I am not grateful to them as well. Here's to you, Aunt Lovelace; to Aunt Darliene and Aunt Gladdie; to Esther and Marietta; to Anne and Andrea, Mary, Susie and Linda . . . the page isn't long enough to name you all. I love you.

Mom, you are a woman of the Word if there ever was one. Thank you for crystallizing truth in teaching moments and keeping the stories of God's faithfulness alive. Thank you for helping me choose stories and refine them, for always being ready to read a chapter or help me puzzle something out. I couldn't have written this without you. And Dad, thank you for always affirming me and challenging me to be who I am created to be, and for showing me the loving fatherhood of God. You believed in this book from the beginning, and your daily encouragement has been a great blessing.

To Mark, my husband and best friend: because of you, I can aim to *be* a woman of the Word. Thank you for your love and support. You read every word, you listened to me in the middle of the night, and you put up with my frustration and absorption and offered wise counsel throughout.

To my kids who live close enough to take part: Abby, your perspective has been invaluable. Chapter by chapter, line by line, you tirelessly and often with little notice read and commented on every draft. Clay, you took time from writing your own papers to help me think through some tough parts. And Zane, you gave up some sweet summer mornings on vacation to weigh in. Thank you all for keeping me real.

To Kelly Wahlquist and Kitty Cleveland, my sisters in this journey: thank you for your friendship and for praying me through. And to the women who gather with me weekly for Bible study and who offered insight as we worked our way through these Scriptures—Kate Camden, Jacki Delaney, Clare Field, Samantha Kelley, Leslie Kelso, Meghan Nulty, Ginny Pellegrino, and Abigail Scogna—may God bless you as you, too, are *becoming women of the Word*.

Philadelphia
February 2, 2019
Feast of the Presentation of the Lord

NOTES

EVE: IN THE BEGINNING, THERE WAS LOVE

1. The *Rite of Christian Initiation of Adults* (RCIA) is the process by which adults inquire into and learn about Catholic teachings and practices and by which they are formally initiated into the Catholic Church.

2. Benedict XVI, *Message of His Holiness Benedict XVI for Lent 2013*, quoting Blaise Pascal, *Pensées*, trans. W. F. Trotter (New York: E. P. Dutton & Co., Inc., 1958), 113.

3. Robert Alter, trans., *The Five Books of Moses: A Translation with Commentary* (New York: W. W. Norton, 2004), 22.

4. For examples of God as "help" (*'ezer*), see Psalms 33:20, 54:4, 70:5, 115:9, and 121:2.

5. See John 14:16, 26; 15:26; and 16:7.

6. In Hebrew, serpent is *nachash*, from the root word meaning "to hiss," that is, whisper a (magic) spell. GodRules.net, accessed November 26, 2017, www.godrules.net/library/strongs2a/heb5172.htm.

7. The Church's teaching on Christ's descent into what we call "hell," the abode of the dead, is summarized in *Catechism*, 631–637.

SARAH: GOD CALLS US TO TRUST

1. The American Friends Service Committee (AFSC) is a Quaker organization that was founded in 1917 to provide an avenue of nonviolent service during World War I. Today it continues to promote peace and justice in the United States.

2. See *Catechism*, 489: "Despite her disobedience, [Eve] receives the promise of a posterity that will be victorious over the evil one, as well as the promise that she will be the mother of all the living. By virtue of this promise, Sarah conceives a son in spite of her old age."

3. See Isaiah 51:1–2, 1 Peter 3:3–6, and Hebrews 11:11.

4. "It is said that . . . Abraham would convert the men, and Sarah, the women" (*Genesis Rabba* 39:14). *Genesis Rabba* is a collection of ancient rabbinical commentaries on the book on Genesis. At another point, the same source says in commenting on Genesis 12:5, "We are told that Abraham took his wife Sarah, and the souls they had gotten in Haran, and they went forth into the land of Canaan. By this is meant the souls that they

had brought away from idolatry and brought to the knowledge of the living God" (*Genesis Rabba* 84). *The Bereshith or Genesis Rabba,* Internet Sacred Text Archive, 66, accessed August 9, 2018, http://www.sacred-texts. com/jud/mhl/mhl05.htm.

5. The seven women recognized in the Jewish tradition as prophets in the Bible are Sarah, Miriam, Deborah, Hannah, Abigail, Huldah, and Esther.

6. Benedict XVI, *Message of His Holiness Benedict XVI for Lent 2013*, http://w2.vatican.va/content/benedict-xvi/en/messages/lent/documents/ hf_ben-xvi_mes_20121015_lent-2013.html.

LEAH AND RACHEL: GOD LONGS TO FILL OUR HEARTS

1. Cornell Capa, "Go Ye and Preach the Gospel," *Life*, January 30, 1956, https://books.google.com/books?id=gT8EAAAAMBAJ&p-g=PA10&dq=life+magazine+jim+elliot#v=onepage&q&f=false.

2. Elisabeth Elliot also tells this story in chapter 16 of her book *These Strange Ashes* (New York: Harper & Row, 1975).

3. *Gateway to Joy* with Elisabeth Elliot was produced by the Good News Broadcasting Association of Lincoln, Nebraska, for nearly thirteen years. The final broadcast was August 31, 2001. Some of the programs can be accessed on BBN, the Bible Broadcasting Network, at https://bbn1. bbnradio.org/english/home/all-programs/gateway-to-joy-elisabeth-elliot.

4. Caryll Houselander, *The Mother of Christ* (London: Sheed & Ward, 1978), 49.

5. You can find the traditional Jewish perspective on Rachel in many places, including this entry on Rachel in the Jewish Encyclopedia: http:// www.jewishencyclopedia.com/articles/12521-rachel. See also Tamar Kadari, "Rachel: Midrash and Aggadah," https://jwa.org/encyclopedia/ article/rachel-midrash-and-aggadah. Both accessed July 12, 2018.

6. See commentary on Genesis 29:31 in Robert Alter, trans., *The Five Books of Moses: A Translation with Commentary* (New York: W. W. Norton, 2008), 156.

7. Ephrath is another name for Bethlehem. During parts of Israel's history, Rachel's tomb was thought to be in Ramah.

8. Blaise Pascal, *Pensées*, trans. W. F. Trotter (New York: E. P. Dutton & Co., Inc., 1958), 113.

MIRIAM: GOD'S LOVE GIVES US WORTH

1. Miriam is a prophet in the sense prophecy is described in Acts 2:11, as expressing "the mighty works of God."

2. John Paul II, *Letter of Pope John Paul II to Women*, Libreria Editrice Vaticana, June 29, 1995, sec. 9, https://w2.vatican.va/content/john-paul-ii/en/letters/1995/documents/hf_jp-ii_let_29061995_women.html. Emphasis in original.

3. Flavius Josephus, *Antiquities of the Jews*, trans. William Whiston, 2.9.3, https://www.biblestudytools.com/history/flavius-josephus/antiquities-jews.

4. Even if that eighty years is a figurative number, when we next see Miriam, she has been waiting for decades.

5. Chana Weisberg, "Miriam: Tambourines of Rebellion," Chabad.org, accessed December 27, 2018, http://www.chabad.org/parshah/article_cdo/aid/248870/jewish/Miriam-Tambourines-of-Rebellion.htm.

6. St. Ambrose, *Concerning Virgins* 1.3.12, cited in notes on Exodus 15:20, *The Ignatius Catholic Study Bible*, Revised Standard Version Second Catholic Edition (San Francisco: Ignatius Press, 2012), 37.

7. "Then it was that Miriam, the sister of Moses, came to her end, having completed her fortieth year since she left Egypt, on the first day of the lunar month Xanthicus. They then made a public funeral for her, at a great expense. She was buried upon a certain mountain, which they call Sin: and when they had mourned for her thirty days, Moses purified the people" (*Antiquities* 4.4.6).

8. Ed Rosenthal, "Parting Is Such Sweet Sorrow," My Jewish Learning, accessed December 27, 2018, https://www.myjewishlearning.com/article/parting-is-such-sweet-sorrow.

RAHAB: GOD IS IN CONTROL OF THE STORMS OF OUR LIVES

1. Julian of Norwich, *Revelations of Divine Love*, trans. Elizabeth Spearing (New York: Penguin, 1998), chap. 31.

2. Benedict XVI, General Audience, Libreria Editrice Vaticana, November 14, 2012, http://w2.vatican.va/content/benedict-xvi/en/audiences/2012/documents/hf_ben-xvi_aud_20121114.html.

3. Benedict XVI, General Audience.

4. Rahab is cited for her faith in James 2:25–26 and Hebrews 11:31.

5. Peter Kreeft, *Fundamentals of the Faith: Essays in Christian Apologetics* (San Francisco: Ignatius Press, 1988), chap. 29.

DEBORAH: GOD CALLS US TO THE LEADERSHIP OF LOVE

1. For comparison, Pharaoh sent six hundred of his best chariots after the Israelites as they fled Egypt (see Exodus 14:17).

2. Origen, *Homilies on Judges (The Fathers of the Church; v. 119)*, trans. Elizabeth Ann Dively Lauro (Washington, DC: The Catholic University of America Press, 2010), 80.

3. Jael isn't the only woman to crush the head of an evil leader. In Judges 9:53, a woman throws an upper millstone on the traitor Abimilech's head and crushes his skull. Most famously, Judith cuts off the head of Holofernes in the book of Judith.

4. Pope John Paul II also writes, "Perhaps more than men, women *acknowledge the person,* because they see persons with their hearts. They see them independently of various ideological or political systems. They see others in their greatness and limitations; they try to go out to them and *help them.* In this way the basic plan of the Creator takes flesh in the history of humanity and there is constantly revealed, in the variety of vocations, that *beauty*—not merely physical, but above all spiritual—which God bestowed from the very beginning on all, and in a particular way on women." John Paul II, *Letter of Pope John Paul II to Women*, Libreria Editrice Vaticana, June 29, 1995, sec. 12, https://w2.vatican.va/content/john-paul-ii/en/letters/1995/documents/hf_jp-ii_let_29061995_women.html. Emphasis in original.

5. Gerald Vann, *Eve and the Gryphon* (Oxford: Blackfriars Publications, 1946), 64. A newer edition of this book, titled *Heart of Compassion: The Vocation of Woman Today*, was published by Sophia Institute Press in 1998.

6. Vann, *Eve and the Gryphon*, 59.

7. Vann, *Eve and the Gryphon*, 70–71.

RUTH: GOD'S KINGDOM HAS ROOM FOR US ALL

1. Robert Frost, "The Road Not Taken" (public domain), from *Poetry Foundation* website, accessed February 7, 2019, https://www.poetryfoundation.org/poems/44272/the-road-not-taken.

2. Shavuot is also called "the Feast of 50 Days" or "Pentecost," for the Greek word for "fiftieth." It falls fifty days after the second day of Passover for Jews, as the Christian Pentecost falls on the seventh Sunday (approximately fifty days) after Easter.

3. Boaz would be their *goel*, or "kinsman-redeemer." This was a person who, as a near relative, was charged with restoring lost rights and avenging wrongs. He had to be a blood relative; must be free himself and so able to help in this way; and must be willing to pay the necessary price. A kinsman-redeemer might be sought to buy back family land, to avenge blood, to redeem a family member from slavery, or to marry the childless widow of a brother in order to continue his family name.

4. Other English translations of *eshet chayil* include "a woman of excellence," "a noble woman," and "a virtuous woman." The Douay-Rheims comes closest to the Jewish tradition's translation with "a valiant woman."

HANNAH: GOD LISTENS TO OUR PRAYERS

1. Augustine, *Letter 130*, 8.17, quoted in *Catechism*, 2737.

2. 1 Samuel 1:19, 2:11. Ramah is also called Ramathaim-zophim (v. 1).

3. Psalms attributed to the sons of Korah are Psalms 42–49, 84, 85, 87, and 88.

4. John Paul II, *Letter of Pope John Paul II to Women*, Libreria Editrice Vaticana, June 29, 1995, sec. 2, https://w2.vatican.va/content/john-paul-ii/en/letters/1995/documents/hf_jp-ii_let_29061995_women.html.

5. Matthew 6:33; Psalm 37:4; see *Catechism*, 2632.

ESTHER: GOD HAS CALLED US "FOR SUCH A TIME AS THIS"

1. Joseph Ratzinger, *Daughter Zion: Meditations on the Church's Marian Belief* (San Francisco: Ignatius Press, 1983), 20–21.

2. Every version of Esther, whether Hebrew, Catholic, or Protestant, numbers the Hebrew chapters the same way, from 1:1 to 10:3. As for the additions: RSVCE follows Jerome's numbering in calling them chapters 10:4–16:24; he appended them at the end of the Hebrew text. NABRE uses the letters A through F instead. Modern translations incorporate the additions into the Hebrew text in their logical location as they were in the Greek, which is why RSVCE begins with chapter 11 and NABRE begins with 1A.

3. See Genesis 50:20. The whole story of Joseph in Genesis 37–50 shows the providential hand of God.

4. A fast would involve crying out to God; see Esther 13:18 and the fasting prayers of Mordecai and Esther in chapters 13 and 14.

5. John Paul II, *Letter of Pope John Paul II to Women*, Libreria Editrice Vaticana, June 29, 1995, sec. 12, https://w2.vatican.va/content/john-paul-ii/en/letters/1995/documents/hf_jp-ii_let_29061995_women.html.

6. Thérèse of Liseiux, *The Story of a Soul*, trans. John Clarke, 3rd ed. (Washington, DC: ICS Publications, 1996), 14–15.

7. Thérèse of Liseiux, *Story of a Soul*, 180.

JUDITH: GOD CREATED OUR BEAUTY FOR GOOD

1. The book of Judith was named among the earliest Christian lists of inspired books and is included in Catholic, though not Protestant, Bibles. Judith was held up as an example to Christians as early as the first century by Pope Clement I (d. AD 99), who praised her courageous love. Her story has inspired artists throughout the centuries.

2. For a man to die at the hand of a woman would mean disgrace in that society (see Judges 9:53–54; 2 Samuel 11:21).

3. Judith 10:4, Latin Vulgate, accessed September 20, 2018, http://www.latinvulgate.com/verse.aspx?t=0&b=18&c=10.

4. See Stephen W. Richey, "Joan of Arc: A Military Appreciation," Saint Joan of Arc Center, accessed September 17, 2018, http://www.stjoan-center.com/military/stephenr.html.

SARAH CHRISTMYER is a Catholic author, speaker, and adjunct faculty member at St. Charles Borromeo Seminary, Philadelphia, Pennsylvania. She is the codeveloper and founding editor of *The Great Adventure* Catholic Bible study program, where she served as director from 2010 to 2013.

She earned a bachelor's degree in English literature from Gordon College in 1981 and a master's degree in theology from St. Charles Borromeo Seminary/School of Theological Studies in 2017.

Christmyer is a member of the board and executive committee of Malvern Retreat House, where she serves as chair of the spiritual programs development committee. She is the author, coauthor, editor, or contributor to more than twenty-five books and bible study programs, including *Gaze Upon Jesus* and *Walk in Her Sandals*. She has blogged for WINE: Women In the New Evangelization, the American Bible Society, and Ascension Press. Christmyer has been a guest on Relevant Radio, Breadbox Media, Radio Maria, Iowa Catholic Radio, and Holy Spirit Radio.

She lives in the Philadelphia, Pennsylvania, area with her family.

www.comintotheword.com
Facebook: SarahChristmyer, Author
Twitter: @SChristmyer
Instagram: @comeintotheword
Pinterest: Come Into the Word—Sarah Christmyer

AVE

For a complete listing of titles from

Ave Maria Press

Sorin Books

Forest of Peace

Christian Classics

visit www.avemariapress.com